Master Bridge

The Allen & Unwin Books on Contract Bridge

ACOL-ITE'S QUIZ by Rhoda Lederer
ALL ABOUT ACOL by Ben Cohen & Rhoda Lederer
BASIC ACOL by Ben Cohen & Rhoda Lederer
YOUR LEAD PARTNER by Ben Cohen & Rhoda Lederer
RIGHT THROUGH THE PACK by Robert Darvas & Norman de V. Hart
CARDS ON THE TABLE by Eric Jannersten, English version by
Rhoda Lederer
THE A.B.C. OF CONTRACT BRIDGE by Ben Cohen &
Rhoda Barrow Lederer
PRECISION BRIDGE by Eric Jannersten, English version by
Rhoda Barrow Lederer
CURRENT CONVENTIONS MADE CLEAR by Ben Cohen
& Rhoda Lederer
MASTER BRIDGE BY QUESTION AND ANSWER
by Alan Truscott: Conversion to British Bidding by
Tony & Rhoda Lederer

Master Bridge
by Question and Answer

ALAN TRUSCOTT

Conversion to British Bidding by
TONY & RHODA LEDERER

London · George Allen & Unwin Ltd
Ruskin House   Museum Street

First published in Great Britain 1973

© The New York Times Company 1971
British Edition © Tony & Rhoda Lederer 1973
© George Allen & Unwin Ltd 1973

ISBN 0 04 793019 5

Printed in Great Britain
in 10 point Linotype Times
by William Clowes & Sons, Limited
London, Beccles and Colchester

Introduction

Bridge is not a game for modest, timid people. If you are shy, quiet and introverted you should stick to knitting, fishing, gardening or solitaire.

Confident, aggressive characters who have faith in themselves are likely to be winners. This is particularly true at the highest levels, where there is a substantial proportion of experts who will admit to being the best in the world.

Unless you are a beginner, and know it, there is a distinct possibility that you overrate your bridge ability. There is also the possibility, a much slighter one, that you underrate yourself.

To find out the truth, perhaps unpalatable, you can test yourself with the quizzes in this book. The questions are not of the text-book type: they are based on situations from actual play. You will be tested in various areas: as opening bidder; as responder; in competitive auctions; in dummy-play; and in defence.

This book, as originally written for the American market, was based on standard bidding methods in the United States. It has been modified by Tony and Rhoda Lederer so that players in Great Britain using either 'Utility' (Kitchen) Two Club or Acol, should be able to achieve a high rating. If you use a specialised bidding system such as Precision Club, your answers will not rate well—although they may be correct according to your methods.

Of course, experts often disagree. The right bid will often be a matter of judgment and style. So if you are an expert, and you are confident that your selected bid deserves more credit than I have given it, please feel free to set up your own rating scale. Give yourself a maximum, if you so wish, and mark me down 80 per cent.

In matters of play and defence, however, the picture changes. Judgment and style become unimportant. Technique and analysis are vital. A particular line of play or defence may provide an extra chance or a superior percentage. A mental reconstruction of one of the unseen hands may indicate the proper plan.

But remember that the play of the hand is not an absolute science. As some of the quizzes demonstrate, there may be a psychological factor. The right play against an expert may be wrong against a beginner, so if your bridge psychology is below the level of your technical skill be warned that your score may suffer.

A word on the quizzes and the ratings. Some questions are harder than others, and some quizzes are harder than others. The maximum award for a question may be as little as five, or it may be as much as 20. Thus the total score possible on each quiz varies according to the number of questions and the total degree of difficulty.

It is suggested that you keep a record of your results on each quiz, and you can give yourself an overall rating at the finish.

If there is a weakness in your game, this book will help you to locate it. Expect to find that you are not quite as good as you thought you were. The problems are tough, especially in the areas of play and defence.

And if your total score is something less than the expert level, do not worry. Comfort yourself with the thought that working through the book will carry you closer to that lofty peak.

If you wish to keep your illusions, or if you do not feel up to the mental exertion needed to attack the quiz problems, skip to the second part of the book. This is made up of 48 of my Sunday bridge columns in *The New York Times*, and they are the raw material on which the quizzes have been based.

Educationalists know that students can, up to a point, improve their scores in educational tests. The same is true in this book. If you choose to read the second part first, thus achieving some understanding of the bidding and play problems involved, you will improve your prospects of a good quiz score.

Whichever way you choose to make use of this book, I guarantee that you will have improved your standard of performance once you have studied it carefully. And that applies whether you are a life master or just out of the novice stage.

This may all sound like toil, tears and sweat, but I think you will get pleasure from this book also: the two are not exclusive.

ALAN TRUSCOTT

*   *   *

We have been at great pains to alter this first class book as little as possible. Clearly, though, Alan Truscott's standard American bidding was going to get British readers nowhere in their efforts to chalk up a good score. When it came to Section 2, 'The Stories Behind the Answers', we have done nothing except, in some cases, explain the bidding and anglicise the spelling and phraseology.

As a small point of interest, Alan Truscott, author of the original book, and Tony Lederer, one of the 'translators', played for England in the same team before Alan Truscott left to settle in the United States in 1962.

TONY AND RHODA LEDERER

Contents

SECTION ONE
THE QUESTIONS
and Answers

The Opening Hand

Opening the bidding is easy—but not as easy as some people think. There are some close decisions, and some unusual situations. And the problems multiply on the next round after partner has responded.

Throughout the bidding sections you can assume that standard bidding methods are being used. Any of the most popular bidding conventions, such as Stayman, Blackwood and Gerber, can be employed where they seem appropriate.

The strong (16–18) no-trump is by no means the standard procedure in Great Britain that it is in the United States, so we have based our modifications on weak (12–14) not vulnerable and 16–18 vulnerable. Even this excludes our standard of 15–17 points when using 'variable' and being vulnerable.

This quiz is not quite as easy as it might seem, so take it slowly.

1. Opponents are vulnerable. What do you bid as dealer with:

♠ A J 5
♥ J 10
♦ A J 10 6 5 2
♣ 5 3

2. Both sides are vulnerable. What do you bid after two passes with:

♠ K 10 9
♥ A K 8 7 4 2
♦ 8 6
♣ 4 2

3. Both sides are vulnerable. What do you open with:

♠ K J 3
♥ A K 7 6 5
♦ K Q
♣ J 10 4

4. Both sides are vulnerable. What do you bid as dealer with:

♠ 4 2
♥ A K Q 10 9 6
♦ -
♣ A K Q 4 3

5. Opponents are vulnerable. What do you open with:

♠ K J 10 6 4
♥ K J
♦ Q 9 7
♣ A K 3

6. Both sides are vulnerable. What do you bid as dealer with:

♠ 5
♥ A K J 10 5 2
♦ Q 6 2
♣ 10 5 2

7. What do you bid after three passes holding:

♠ J
♥ A 4 2
♦ A K 7 4
♣ A K Q 9 8

8. Both sides are vulnerable. What do you bid as dealer with:

♠ 8 6
♥ -
♦ 7 3
♣ A Q J 9 8 6 5 4 2

9. Both sides are vulnerable. What do you bid as dealer with:

♠ A K 8 5 3
♥ 7
♦ A K 8 4
♣ A Q 4

10. Your side is vulnerable. What do you bid following a pass on your right with:

♠ Q 8
♥ A J
♦ K 6 2
♣ A K Q 9 7 5

11. What do you bid as dealer with:

♠ A 9 7 4
♥ K 10 6 5
♦ K 7 6
♣ A J

12. Not vulnerable. what do you bid after three passes holding:

♠ Q 7 6
♥ A Q J
♦ A 6 5 4 2
♣ K 3

13. Both sides are vulnerable. What do you bid as dealer with:

♠ K
♥ K Q 9 8 6 5 2
♦ 8 6 3
♣ J 5

14. Opponents are vulnerable, you are not. What do you bid in second position with:

♠ K J 10 9 5 4
♥ 5
♦ K Q J 10 8 6
♣ -

15. Both sides are vulnerable. What do you open with:

♠ A 8 2
♥ J 10 2
♦ K Q J 10 3
♣ 6 4

16. Both sides are vulnerable. What do you open with:

♠ A K 8 4 3
♥ K
♦ A 9
♣ A 9 6 5 3

17. Both sides are vulnerable. What do you do after two passes with:

♠ Q 6 5
♥ A Q J 8
♦ 9 7 3
♣ A 9 4

18. You open one club in fourth seat and your partner responds one diamond. What would you rebid with:

♠ J
♥ A 4 2
♦ A K 7 4
♣ A K Q 9 8

19. You open one spade as dealer and your partner raises to two spades. What would you rebid with:

♠ K 10 9 6 5
♥ -
♦ A K 7 5
♣ A K Q 6

20. You open one spade as dealer and your partner responds two diamonds. What would you rebid with:

♠ A Q J 6 3 2
♥ A K 5
♦ Q J 6
♣ J

21. You open one spade in second seat and your partner responds two diamonds. What would you rebid with:

♠ K J 9 7 4 3
♥ K J 10 8
♦ A 10
♣ A

22. You open one spade as dealer and your partner raises to two spades. What do you rebid with:

♠ A K 8 5 3
♥ 7
♦ A K 8 4
♣ A Q 4

23. You open one heart in third position and your partner responds one no-trump. What do you rebid with:

♠ K J 7 2
♥ A K 8 6 3
♦ A 10 4
♣ A

24. You open one spade as dealer, and your partner responds two clubs. What do you rebid with:

♠ A 9 8 6 2
♥ K 8 5
♦ A
♣ A 10 9 2

25. Both sides are vulnerable. You have opened one club—one diamond would have been a better alternative—on the following hand:

♠ 9 4 2
♥ K Q 7
♦ A 10 4 2
♣ A 5 2

Your partner has responded one diamond, and you have chosen to rebid one no-trump rather than raise diamonds.
(a) What do you do when your partner now bids four clubs?
(b) And what will your next bid be if he follows with five clubs?

26. You are vulnerable and dealer passes on your right. What do you bid with:

♠ K 3
♥ K 8 6
♦ K Q 2
♣ Q 9 7 6 3

27. You open one spade with this hand:

♠ A K 8 5 4 2
♥ 5
♦ 10 7 3 2
♣ A 4

Your partner responds two clubs and you rebid two spades. What should you do when he rebids three no-trumps?

28. You have opened one club with the following hand:

♠ Q 8
♥ A J
♦ K 6 2
♣ A K Q 9 7 5

What do you do next when your partner responds three no-trumps?

29. The bidding has gone:

West	North	East	South
Pass	1 ♠	Pass	2 ♣
Pass	2 NT	Pass	3 ♦
Pass	3 ♠	Pass	4 ♦
Pass	?		

What do you bid now with:

♠ A 9 7 6 3 2
♥ K 8 7
♦ A Q
♣ Q 5

30. Neither side is vulnerable. Using five-card majors, you bid one diamond with:

♠ A 9 7 4
♥ K 10 6 5
♦ K 7 6
♣ A J

Your left-hand opponent overcalls one no-trump and there are two passes. What do you do now?

31. You are vulnerable, the opponents are not. You deal and bid one spade, and there is an overcall of two hearts. Your partner bids three spades (encouraging but not forcing) and your right-hand opponent bids four hearts. What do you do with:

♠ A 10 5 4 2
♥ A 2
♦ A 7 6 3
♣ 10 8

32. You open one heart, neither side vulnerable. There follows a two-club overcall, a two-spade bid and a pass. What do you bid now with:

♠ A 10 6
♥ K Q 8 7 3
♦ A
♣ 10 8 5 4

33. Opponents are vulnerable. In second seat you open three clubs and there is an overcall of three hearts. Your partner's three-spade bid is passed and you have:

♠ J 3
♥ J
♦ J 9 5
♣ K J 10 8 6 3 2

What do you call?

34. Opponents are vulnerable, you are not. As West, you bid one spade following dealer's pass, and are doubled. Your partner passes. What do you do now when your right-hand opponent (South) jumps to two no-trumps and you have:

♠ K J 10 9 5 4
♥ 5
♦ K Q J 10 8 6
♣ –

Answers

1. One diamond, 5 points; pass, 3.
On borderline hands the possession of aces and tens can be a crucial factor. On this hand you have four in aces and tens, so you are worth a one-bid. The strength in the diamond suit is also a factor. With a weaker suit one might pass.   (See hand 13)

2. One heart, 5 points; two hearts (weak), 4.
To pass with such a hand in third seat would be somewhat cowardly. As the hand has defensive strength as well as a long suit, one heart is fractionally preferable to a weak two-bid.

(See hand 5)

3. One heart, 5 points; one no-trump, 3.
A close decision, and most players would probably bid one heart simply because they have a five-card major. There is no objection to this, as whatever partner responds, you have a sensible rebid. Over any suit response you can rebid two no-trumps.

(See hand 27)

4. Two hearts (playing Acol strong two bids) or two clubs (playing 'Utility' or 'Kitchen'), 5.
You don't count points on this sort of hand—only playing tricks, of which you have eleven. You want to be in game even opposite to a yarborough, so you say so immediately by opening two hearts and, if partner responds with the negative two no-trumps, you rebid a forcing four clubs, demanding preference to four hearts or a raise to five clubs. There are no possible grounds for opening one heart on this hand, as you will then never be able to show your great playing strength in the subsequent bidding.

(See hand 34)

5. One spade, 5 points; one no-trump (playing 'strong') 2.

A very close decision, and experts would have divided opinions. If the suit were hearts, the argument for one no-trump would be slightly stronger because of the potential rebid problem after a response of one spade. (See hand 45)

6. Two hearts (weak), or one heart, 5 points; three hearts or pass, 2.

Compare this with question 2. The heart suit is stronger, there is less outside strength, and there is more reason to fear an opposing spade contract. So players using a weak two-bid may score well here. To bid three hearts vulnerable on this hand could be an expensive outing. (See hand 22)

7. One club, 5 points; two clubs, 3.

In this borderline area between one-bids and forcing bids, the criterion is the prospect of game opposite a weak hand. If partner cannot respond to one club the chances of game are very slight. A forcing opening (strong two or artificial two clubs, according to style) would have much more to recommend it with a major suit to bid. (See hand 30)

8. Five clubs, 5 points; four clubs, 2.

You have better than eight playing tricks, and no defence. If the opponents can double you and collect 800 they may have missed a slam. Four clubs would be timid. (See hand 3)

9. One spade, 5 points; two clubs (strong artificial) or two spades (strong two-bid), 2.

This is obviously a close decision. The danger of missing a game by having one spade passed out seems less than the danger of causing partner to overestimate slam prospects by opening with a forcing bid, or reaching a hopeless game opposite a weak misfitting hand. (See hand 35)

10. One club, 10 points; two no-trumps, 5.

If partner makes any free response you can jump to three no-trumps. The solid club suit, presumably worth six tricks in play, should make this a good contract. The doubleton spade queen should not be regarded as a liability, and if partner has, say, ♠ A x x or ♠ K x x, a no-trump contract should be played from

the queen side. The routine bid of one club will cause no rebid
problems. (See hand 33)

11. One heart, 10; one spade, 5; one diamond, 3.
This is an awkward hand, but a one heart opening will ensure
that neither a heart nor a spade contract is missed, whilst if
partner responds with two of a minor you can rebid two no-
trumps. For those using five-card majors, a one-diamond opening is acceptable. One club with only two cards in the suit is
quite unsound. (See hand 10)

**12. One diamond, 10 points; or (for strong no-trump bidders)
one no-trump, 8.**
If you are playing a strong no-trump you have no problem on
this hand, but being non-vulnerable, you are too strong for this
bid. A one diamond opening leaves you with no rebid problems,
as you can bid two no-trumps over any simple response from
partner. (See hand 11)

**13. Three hearts, 10 points; two hearts (weak), 7; one heart or
pass, 3.**
A strong seven-card suit and insufficient defensive strength for a
one-bid is just about right for a vulnerable three-bid.

(See hand 21)

**14. One spade, 10 points; one diamond or four spades, 5; three
spades, 3.**
With such freak distribution it is slightly better to open one
spade in the hope of being able to bid diamonds later, than to
pre-empt, losing all hope of showing diamonds. If a pre-emptive
bid is made, four spades is rather better than three, but even
four does not do justice to the great playing strength of the hand.

(See hand 39)

15. Pass, 10 points; one diamond, 5.
Even allowing for the possession of two tens and a strong suit,
this hand is just short of an opening. One diamond would be
acceptable in third seat but not as dealer. (See hand 44)

16. One club, 10 points; one spade, 5.
With two black suits of equal length you should open one club.
If this is followed by two successive rebids in spades the best

distributional picture is given. One spade serves to shut out the opponents to some extent, but this seems less important.

(See hand 16)

17. One heart, 10 points; one club, 5.

In third seat it is much better to bid one heart, the suit you want led if you defend, than to bid a three-card club suit. One heart would be slightly inferior in first or second seat because of the rebid problem after a two-level response in a minor suit. This does not arise after a third-hand opening, because the response can be passed. Only the vulnerability rules out the best opening of all—one no-trump.

(See hand 18)

18. Two hearts, 10 points; four no-trumps or five diamonds, 5.

The standard bid is a jump switch to two hearts, a bid that sometimes has to be made in a three-card suit. A jump to three diamonds or three clubs would be quite wrong because partner could pass: once you know your side has a game never make a bid below game that your partner can pass.

(See hand 30)

19. Five spades, 10 points; four hearts, 8; three diamonds or three clubs, 3.

When there are at least two unbid suits, a bid of five in the agreed trump suit means 'bid six if you have strong trumps partner'. It implies a lack of concern about controls outside the trump suit. (If there is only one unbid suit, the bid asks about control in that suit.) As after a single raise to two spades a bid of three hearts would be a (forcing) trial bid, a jump to four hearts is used by many experts to show trump agreement, a void in the suit jump-bid (hearts), and slam prospects.

(See hand 1)

20. Three spades, 10 points; two hearts, 5; four spades or four diamonds, 4.

Three spades gives a good description of the hand which is just below strength for a strong two, so there is no need for anything fancy. With a fit in diamonds you have something in reserve, but that can wait.

(See hand 4)

21. Two hearts, 10 points; three spades, 6; three hearts, 3.

Whether or not a simple rebid in a new suit is forcing is a matter of system. In some systems it is forcing, in Acol it is not. Playing

Acol, therefore, you risk a pass by bidding two hearts if partner is absolutely minimum for his two diamonds and has a preference for hearts. If you rebid two spades the bidding may end, and if you follow this with three hearts you imply a sub-minimum 6–4 hand. The immediate jump to three spades shows the six-card suit and the strength of the hand, but suggests that you do not have hearts to bid. (See hand 32)

22. Three diamonds, or three clubs, 10 points; four diamonds or four clubs, 7; four spades, 3.
An exploring move in a minor suit is called for. A direct jump to game, giving up on slam chances, is too cowardly.

(See hand 35)

23. Two spades, 10 points; three spades, 3.
Your combined assets seem to justify a game bid, but there may not be a satisfactory place to play the hand. Two spades is a reverse showing great strength, and most experts consider it forcing. Even if partner can pass, the chance that he will do so is slight—and if that happens there may not be a game. Partner is unlikely to have a four-card spade suit when he responds one no-trump. Three spades is justified in terms of strength, but crowds the auction to such an extent that it may be hard to determine the best game contract. (See hand 48)

24. Four clubs, 10 points; three clubs, 5.
With a powerful fit and excellent controls a bid of only three clubs would be over-timid. A raise to three clubs does not show any additional strength (although some old-fashioned text-books may say it does). Four clubs shows at least a 5–4 distribution in the black suits. (See hand 9)

25. (a) Four spades, 10 points.
Partner's four-club bid is the Gerber Convention, asking how many aces you hold. You respond on the Blackwood principle. Four diamonds would show no ace, so four spades shows two.
   (b) Five hearts, 5 points.
The follow-up of five clubs asks for kings in similar fashion. You must bid five hearts to show one king. (See hand 29)

26. One club or (for weak no-trump bidders), one no-trump, 10 points; pass, 5 points.

Some cautious experts would pass, discouraged by the lack of aces, but 13 points is enough to open. Weak no-trump bidders *must* bid 1 NT, for they will have no good rebid if they open one club. (See hand 38)

27. Pass, 10 points; four spades, 5.

If your partner is a good player, he is not interested in playing four spades. He should have the unbid suits well-stopped, and he may be short in spades—perhaps a singleton or a void.

(See hand 2)

28. Four clubs, 10 points; six no-trumps, 8; six clubs, 6.*

Four clubs is forcing, as it removes an existing game contract to one below game level. Partner would be well advised to treat it as a Gerber bid, asking for aces. The chance that we are missing two aces is very slight, for our 19 points plus partner's presumed 13 makes 32 out of 40. But there is no need to take the chance. Even if we have all four aces in the combined hands we should not consider a grand slam, which can hardly be better than a finesse chance. As between no-trumps and clubs, we should certainly pick no-trumps at any form of duplicate. In rubber bridge the decision would be close. (See hand 33)

29. Six clubs, 10 points; five clubs, 5.

Your partner has shown slam prospects with five diamonds and six clubs. You have eight points in his suits and an outside ace, so your hand is excellently suited to a slam. The slam should be in clubs, knowing what you do about your partner's distribution, so just bid it. In Great Britain most Norths would prefer to rebid two spades, but the same final contract should be reached as South's bidding marks him as 6–5 in clubs and diamonds.

(See hand 8)

30. Pass, 10 points.

You have little in reserve for your opening bid. It would be a bad mistake to take any further action. Your partner must be

---

* No rating for four no-trumps. which would be a natural slam invitation, not Blackwood. We cannot afford to risk being out of slam.

weak—with fair strength he would have doubled one no-trump
—and he may have almost nothing.   (See hand 10)

31. Double, 10 points; four spades or pass, 3.
Your partner should have about 11 points, so you are short of
the high-card strength needed for game. But your three aces suggest that the opponents will be defeated in four hearts.

(See hand 20)

32. Three spades, 10 points; four spades, 5.
Partner must have at least a five-card spade suit, and is probably
short in clubs, so prospects of game are quite good. Nevertheless,
three spades is enough with this minimum hand. A jump to four
spades might induce partner to reach for a slam.   (See hand 40)

33. Four spades, 10 points; four clubs, 5.
Three spades is forcing, so you may not pass. Your partner
already knows about your club suit, so try not to tell the same
story twice. He must have a very strong spade suit—probably a
six-carder—so the doubleton jack is sufficient support.

(See hand 28)

34. Four diamonds, 10 points; three diamonds or five diamonds, 5.
As South would pass the double with a hand containing high-
card strength, any other action suggests distributional power
rather than high cards. Three diamonds does not convey ade-
quately the great playing-strength of the hand. Five diamonds
goes too far, since it rules out a contract of four spades. Four
diamonds is about right.   (See hand 39)

Awards

260–300	OUTSTANDING
200–250	VERY GOOD INDEED
150–190	ABOVE AVERAGE
100–140	BELOW AVERAGE
50–90	FAIR
0–40	POOR

The Responding
Hand

The responder is rather more likely to have difficult decisions than the opener. Should he describe his own hand, or should he invite the opener to describe his? Do the combined hands offer prospects of slam, or game, or just a part-score?

The first three bids may not solve the problem. The responder may still be in doubt, and he must bear in mind what his partner's bids have meant, and how much reserve strength he has of his own.

This quiz is a little harder than its predecessor. You will have to work to achieve an equally good result, but you should have a fine opportunity to improve on a bad one.

1. Your partner opens one club in fourth seat. What would you respond with:

♠ K 7 5 3
♥ K J 6 5
♦ Q J 8 3
♣ 3

2. Your partner deals and bids one spade using five-card majors. What would you respond with:

♠ Q J 4
♥ K Q 9 8 3
♦ J
♣ 9 8 4 2

3. Your partner opens one club in third seat. What would you respond with:

♠ 7
♥ Q 3
♦ A K 10 7 2
♣ 9 8 7 6 3

4. Your partner opens with one club in second seat. What would you respond with:

♠ K J 5
♥ K Q 10
♦ A 9 8 7 3
♣ 10 2

5. Your partner opens one club. What would you respond with:

♠ A K Q
♥ A 4
♦ K J 8 5 3
♣ K Q J

6. Your partner opens one club as dealer. You hold:

♠ 9 8
♥ A Q
♦ Q 4 3
♣ A K J 10 9 2

(a) What would you respond?
(b) What would you respond with a part-score of 40?

7. Both sides are vulnerable. What do you respond with the following hand when your partner opens one heart in third seat?

♠ Q 10 5 4
♥ A 10 9
♦ 6
♣ K J 10 7 2

8. Both sides are vulnerable. What do you respond when your partner bids one diamond as dealer and you hold:

♠ J 9 4
♥ A 6 3
♦ 9 6 2
♣ A Q 10 9

9. Neither side vulnerable. Your partner bids one spade in second position. What do you respond with:

♠ 9 5
♥ A 8 4 3
♦ A Q 7 5
♣ A K 8

10. Neither side vulnerable. Your partner has opened one diamond, and your right-hand opponent has made a weak jump overcall of two hearts. What do you bid with:

♠ K 5 3
♥ A Q 6
♦ 6 5 4
♣ J 7 4 2

11. Both sides vulnerable. Your partner has opened one heart, and your right-hand opponent has jumped to three diamonds (strong). What do you bid with:

♠ A Q 10 8 3
♥ 10 7 3
♦ 9 7 2
♣ Q 4

12. Neither side vulnerable. You deal and pass, and your partner's one-club bid is doubled. What do you bid now with:

♠ A 8
♥ J 7 5
♦ A 8 6 5 4 2
♣ 10 3

13. Neither side is vulnerable. Your partner bids one heart in second seat and the next player bids one spade. What do you bid now with:

♠ Q 8 2
♥ K 7 6 3
♦ 8 6 2
♣ A J 4

14. Your partner has opened one spade, and has rebid two spades when you have responded two clubs. What do you rebid with:

♠ Q 9
♥ K J 4
♦ A 5
♣ Q J 10 8 7 2

15. Your partner has opened one club, and rebid three diamonds over your two-diamond response. What would you rebid with:

♠ A K Q
♥ A 4
♦ K J 8 5 3
♣ K Q J

16. Your partner has opened one diamond and rebid the suit when you responded two clubs. What do you rebid with:

♠ K 6 3
♥ A 9 8 4
♦ 3
♣ A J 8 4 2

17. Both vulnerable. You pass in second seat with:

♠ K 7
♥ 10 9 7 6 4 2
♦ K J 10 3
♣ 8

Your partner opens one diamond and raises your one-heart response to two. What now?

18. You respond two clubs to one spade with:

> ♠ J 10
> ♥ -
> ♦ K J 10 6 3
> ♣ A K J 10 7 6

What do you do next when your partner rebids two no-trumps?

19. Your partner has opened one spade and has rebid two hearts when you have responded two diamonds. What do you rebid with:

> ♠ A Q 8
> ♥ 5
> ♦ K J 9 7 5
> ♣ Q 9 8 5

20. Your partner opens one no-trump, showing 16–18 points. What do you respond after an opponent's pass with:

> ♠ 9 5 3
> ♥ 6 4
> ♦ A K 10 8 2
> ♣ 9 8 5

21. You are North and the bidding has gone:

East	South	West	North
Pass	1 ♣	Pass	2 ♦
Pass	3 ♦	Pass	4 N.T.
Pass	5 ♥	Pass	5 N.T.
Pass	6 ♦	Pass	?

Your hand is:

> ♠ A K Q
> ♥ A 4
> ♦ K J 8 5 3
> ♣ K Q J

What do you bid now?

22. You are South and the bidding has gone:

North	East	South	West
1 ♠	Pass	2 ♣	Pass
4 ♣	Pass	4 NT	Pass
5 ♠	Pass	?	

What do you bid now with:

♠ K Q 5
♥ A 9 4
♦ 9 4 2
♣ K Q J 7

23. Neither side vulnerable. The bidding has gone:

North	East	South	West
1 ♥	2 ♣	2 ♠	Pass
4 ♠	Pass	?	

What do you do now as South holding:

♠ K Q J 9 5 4 3
♥ J
♦ Q 7 2
♣ K 3

24. You have responded two diamonds to one spade (opponents are silent) with the following hand:

♠ K 10 7
♥ 6
♦ K 9 7 3 2
♣ A K Q 7

What do you do next when your partner rebids three spades?

25. Your partner opens two no-trumps, showing 21–22 points, and you have:

♠ J 6
♥ A J 8 4 2
♦ J 6 5 3 2
♣ J

(a) What do you respond when your right-hand opponent passes?
(b) Would your decision be affected if your partner's bid showed 22–24 points?

26. Your partner opens one no-trump. showing 16–18 points. The opponents are silent. What do you respond with:

♠ 7 4
♥ J 2
♦ A 10 9
♣ A K Q 9 7 3

27. Your partner opens one no-trump, showing 16–18 points. What do you respond, after an opponent's pass, with:

♠ 6 4
♥ A K 7 3
♦ A 10 6
♣ A Q 7 2

28. Your opponents are vulnerable and your partner opens in third position with three diamonds. After a cue bid of four diamonds on your right, what do you bid with:

♠ Q J 10
♥ 4 2
♦ J 6 4 3
♣ K 8 4 2

Answers

1. One diamond, 10 points; one heart, 8; one spade, 3.
The general rule with four-card suits is to keep the bidding low when responding. One diamond gives the opener a chance to bid either major suit. One heart is almost as good, but virtually rules out the chance—admittedly not too likely—of playing the hand in diamonds.   (See hand 30)

2. Two spades, 10 points; two hearts, 5.
Two spades is a very slight underbid. Two hearts is a slight over-bid. If you choose the overbid, you will not know whether to raise if your partner rebids his spades. Once you have bid two spades, it will be easy to bid if your partner makes a move towards game.   (See hand 1)

3. Two diamonds, 10 points; three clubs, 8; one diamond or four clubs, 5.
The jump switch by a passed hand implies a fit with the opener as well as a long, strong suit. (A hand containing a long, strong suit but no fit would probably have qualified for a weak two-bid originally.) If the opener makes a simple rebid in his suit he suggests a sub-minimum hand and the responder should nor-mally pass. In this case the jump switch is much more descriptive than the possible alternatives.   (See hand 5)

4. Three no-trumps, 10 points; one diamond, 8.
With both major suits well stopped it is slightly better to show your partner you have a balanced hand and an opening bid by jumping to three no-trumps than to make the routine response of one diamond. A limited, descriptive bid should usually be preferred to a waiting bid which leaves partner in the dark.
                                                    (See hand 33)

5. Two diamonds, 10 points.
Two diamonds shows slam potential. The suit is a little thin for a force, but with 23 points there is no alternative.

(See hand 29)

6. (a) One diamond, 10 points; four no-trumps or six clubs, 5; two hearts, 3; (b) Four no-trumps, 10 points; six clubs, 9; four or five clubs, 5.
One would normally like to make a forcing bid, but three clubs is a non-forcing limit bid, and probably the best alternative is a waiting bid of one diamond. If you feel you must force, two hearts is the only sensible alternative.

Neither of these actions is acceptable with a part-score of 40 because the bidding might die. A direct gamble in the direction of slam seems the least evil. (See hand 25)

7. Three hearts, 10 points; three clubs, 7; two clubs or one spade, 5.
As you have passed already, a simple black suit response might be passed. You are prepared to play in a four-three heart fit if needs must. The best alternative is a jump to three clubs showing a heart fit and a maximum pass. Two clubs would score more if used as the 'Drury Convention'. (A two-club response by a passed hand to a major-suit opening asks the opener to show a sub-minimum hand by bidding two diamonds and otherwise to make any other bid.) (See hand 26)

8. Two clubs, 10 points; two no-trumps, 8.
Two clubs in response to one diamond nearly always shows at least a five-card club suit, but this hand is the exception. You have a no-trump hand with the values for two no-trumps, but the spade situation makes this slightly dangerous. So temporise with two clubs. (See hand 44)

9. Three diamonds, 10 points; three clubs, 8; two diamonds, 5.
A jump switch normally suggests a very strong suit or a hand that fits opener's suit. However, a hand with slam prospects may best be bid via a jump switch in some circumstances. By jumping to three diamonds here you can leave subsequent moves toward slam to partner. If you make the response of two diamonds it may be hard to suggest a slam without going unsafely beyond the game level. (See hand 46)

10. Two no-trumps, 10 points; two no-trumps or two hearts, 8; double, 5.

Two no-trumps is the ideal bid. It is non-forcing, suggesting a balanced hand with the hearts stopped at least once and about 10–12 high-card points. The alternatives are markedly inferior. The double is poor whatever meaning is assigned to it. The hearts are not good enough for a penalty double, and for a negative double (favoured by many tournament players) a four-card spade suit would be required. (See hand 19)

11. Three hearts, 10 points; pass, 3.

A raise at the three-level made 'under pressure'—i.e. when an opponent's bid has ruled out a single raise—shows a hand in the upper range for a normal single raise. The point-count is likely to be 8–10. West need not worry about the quality of his heart support. Even if the partnership agreement allows bids in four-card majors, the jump to three diamonds vastly increases the probability that East has at least a five-card suit. (See hand 21)

12. Two diamonds, 10 points; redouble, 3.

One diamond is unacceptable as it is used as a weak rescue bid. Redouble generally implies willingness to double the final enemy contract, but you cannot do this if doubler's partner responds in a major. Two diamonds shows a hand with a good suit of its own which is unsuitable for a redouble, so is the best choice here. (See hand 23)

13. Three hearts, 10 points; two hearts, 8; two no-trumps, 5; one no-trump, 3.

The limit bids are used in exactly the same way over an intervening bid as if there had been no interference. Without the one-spade bid you would bid three hearts, so bid it now. One no-trump is given 3 marks not because it has any merit, but because it would be so much worse to pass. (See hand 14)

14. Four spades, 10 points; three hearts, 5; three no-trumps, 3.

Partner should have a six-card suit or a strong five-card suit in this situation. So four spades should be safe, and three no-trumps may be wrecked by a diamond lead. The second choice is not three no-trumps but three hearts, hoping to steer partner into bidding three no-trumps. If hearts are raised, an unlikely event, we can revert to spades. (See hand 2)

15. Four no-trumps, 10 points; five no-trumps, 9; six no-trumps or seven no-trumps, 5.

Four no-trumps is the Blackwood Convention, asking how many aces partner has. This will help you to decide whether to bid six or seven. Five no-trumps conventionally forces six and invites seven. so it is about right quantitatively. No marks for four clubs as in Britain it would merely be showing club support.

(See hand 29)

16. Two hearts, 10 points; two no-trumps, 8.

You are certainly worth a move towards game. Two hearts is descriptive and forcing. There might be a four-four heart fit, which is why the bid is slightly preferable to two no-trumps.

(See hand 13)

17. Four hearts, 10 points; three hearts, 7.

Although you have only seven high-card points, the double fit is grounds for great optimism. You hope to lose only two tricks in the black suits, and on partner's bidding there must be a good chance to lose only one trick in the red suits. Even if you go down the result may not be bad: the opponents will have missed a part-score in spades or even a game. (See hand 6)

18. Three diamonds, 10 points.

You intend to follow with four diamonds, showing considerable strength and completing the picture of a 5-6 distribution in the minor suits. (See hand 8)

19. Three spades, 10 points; three clubs, 8; four spades, 2.

Three spades shows three-card spade support as the suit has not yet been rebid (i.e. not necessarily a five-card suit). It is a non-forcing jump or preference bid. Four spades would give the impression of four-card spade support in a hand worth a delayed game raise. (See hand 32)

20. Two no-trumps, 10 points; three no-trumps, or pass, 5.

The long, strong diamond suit makes this hand the equivalent of most hands with eight or nine points, so the standard raise to two no-trumps is in order. Any attempt to play in diamonds would be poor judgment with such a balanced hand, but a gambling raise to three no-trumps would not be completely out of line. (See hand 45)

21. Seven no-trumps, 10 points; six no-trumps, 7.
South is marked with the minor-suit aces and the heart king, and must have two, three or four points in addition. If those points include the diamond queen the grand slam is a lay-down. If not, the grand slam will be at worst on a finesse, so the gamble is a reasonable one.

An expert might well bid six hearts or six spades, in the hope that partner will realise that the diamond queen is the crucial card for the purposes of a grand slam. This cannot hurt with an expert partner, although it might confuse a player of limited experience. If you made one of these bids, take full points.
(See hand 29)

22. Five no-trumps, 10 points; seven clubs, 8; six clubs, 6; six spades, 3.
It is highly likely that your partner has five spades and four clubs, in which case a club contract will be more productive than a spade contract. The 4-4 fit is generally better than the 5-3 fit, and with every card in your hand pulling its weight there should be excellent chances of making 13 tricks in clubs. Your partner must have something beside three aces to justify his four-club bid. (See hand 9)

23. Four no-trumps, 10 points; five clubs, 7; pass, 3.
There is a reasonable chance that partner has three aces, in which case six spades should be a good contract. This breaks the rule that a Blackwood bidder should not have two quick losers in an unbid suit, but there is no attractive alternative. The cue-bid of five clubs would suggest the ace but might work out all right. To give up on slam chances would be a trifle cowardly.
(See hand 40)

24. Four no-trumps, 10 points; five hearts or four clubs, 3.
This is the ideal hand for Blackwood. You know you will play in spades, and you have a wealth of second-round controls. Only the absence of two aces will stop you bidding a slam.
(See hand 4)

25. (a) Three hearts, 10 points.

This bid indicates a five-card heart suit and values at least for a game. The opener can sign off in three no-trumps with a doubleton heart; raise to four hearts; or invite a heart slam with a minor-suit cue-bid at the four-level if his hand is particularly suitable for a 12-trick contract.

A Stayman bid or Baron bid of three clubs would be a bad mistake, for you would not know what to do after a three-spade rebid by partner.

(b) No. Still bid three hearts, 5 points.

The same response is right if the opening is 22–24 points. Now the slam chances are a little better, and you can plan to persevere with four diamonds if your partner denies heart support by rebidding three no-trumps. If he then bids four no-trumps—a natural bid, of course—the hand is a misfit and you give up.

(See hand 36)

26. Six no-trumps or four clubs (Gerber), 10 points; three clubs (strong) or six clubs, 8; two clubs, 4.

Six no-trumps is highly likely to be the right contract although it will not hurt to bid four clubs en route to guard against the slight chance that two aces are missing. (Even if they are missing, the opponents may have trouble cashing them.) The chance of a sound grand slam contract is slight, and exploring will help the defence. No-trumps should be better than a club slam because the lead will come round to the strong hand.   (See hand 27)

27. Five no-trumps, 10 points; two clubs (Stayman), 8; six no-trumps, 7; three clubs, 5.

In the U.S.A. five no-trumps would be the expert bid, if you have a knowledge of partner. It guarantees six no-trumps and suggests a grand slam. If the opener has more than a minimum hand he should show any respectable four-card suit at the six-level. Our final contract may, therefore, be six no-trumps, seven clubs, or seven no-trumps.

A Stayman bid may locate a heart fit if there is one, but it will not help much in exploring grand slam possibilities, which a direct raise to slam abandons completely. Three clubs is less good, not only because it suggests a long club suit, but also because there is room for misunderstanding: many good players regard a three-club response as pre-emptive in this situation.

(See hand 42)

Note. Most players in Britain would take the five no-trump bid as a demand to go to six no-trumps and an invitation to go to seven no-trumps on a maximum opener, and would not show a four-card suit on the way. This could land the partnership in seven no-trumps missing an ace, so we should prefer a direct six no-trumps to carry maximum marks.

28. Five diamonds, 10 points; four hearts, four spades or four no-trumps, 8; six diamonds, 5.
An honest raise to five diamonds should create enough problems for the opponents. Six diamonds is a little too much, since it may cost 700 or 900 points with no slam available for the opponents, but attempts to confuse the issue at the four-level are acceptable. No score for a double or a passive pass.

(See hand 38)

Awards

250–300	OUTSTANDING
200–240	VERY GOOD INDEED
150–190	ABOVE AVERAGE
100–140	BELOW AVERAGE
50–90	FAIR
0–40	POOR

Competitive Bidding

The toughest problems in bidding arise when both sides are taking part in the auction. Experts constantly find themselves faced with unfamiliar situations in this area, which they must solve by a combination of judgment and experience.

Some players never achieve any proficiency in this area, for rules are of little help. But if you go astray you can learn from your mistakes by making an effort.

So do not worry if you do not score well on this quiz. But make sure that you understand the principles involved in the answer, so that you can improve your performance at the table.

1. Neither side vulnerable. The dealer on your right, who is using five-card majors, opens one diamond. What do you bid with:

♠ K Q 3
♥ A J 2
♦ Q 9 2
♣ K 9 7 2

2. Neither side vulnerable. The dealer on your right opens one diamond. What do you bid with:

♠ 7 4
♥ K 10 9 5 4 3
♦ A Q 7 3
♣ 8

3. The opponents are vulnerable. The dealer on your right opens one spade. What do you bid with:

♠ K Q J
♥ K J 10 9 8 7 3
♦ 10
♣ Q 6

4. The opponents are vulnerable. The dealer on your right bids one diamond. What do you bid with:

♠ K J 10 9 8 7 6 5
♥ K
♦ J 7 6 3
♣ -

5. Opponents vulnerable. After a pass from your partner and one spade on your right what do you bid with:

♠ 7
♥ A K 10 9 7 3
♦ A 4
♣ K Q 9 8

6. Both sides are vulnerable. The dealer on your right bids one heart. What do you bid with:

♠ 5
♥ 4
♦ A K Q J 10 4
♣ A K 8 3 2

7. Your side only is vulnerable. After the dealer on your right bids one heart what do you bid with:

♠ A K Q 9 7 4 3
♥ 10 9 8
♦ 10 6
♣ 2

8. Neither side is vulnerable. After your right-hand opponent has bid one club in third seat what do you bid with:

♠ K 9 7 4
♥ K Q 10 3
♦ K 10
♣ K 9 4

9. Neither side is vulnerable. The dealer on your right bids one no-trump (16–18 pts). What do you bid with:

♠ A Q 10 9 8 7
♥ A
♦ A K J 4
♣ 6 5

10. Both sides are vulnerable. The dealer on your right bids one club. What do you bid with:

♠ A Q 8
♥ A K Q J
♦ Q J 10 9 8 2
♣ -

11. The opponents are vulnerable. Your partner overcalls dealer's bid of one diamond with four spades, and your right-hand opponent passes. What do you bid with:

♠ A 4 3 2
♥ A 10 5 4 3 2
♦ A 5 4
♣ -

12. Your side only is vulnerable. You deal, and your one-diamond bid is followed by two passes. What do you call when your right-hand opponent bids one heart and you have:

♠ A K 10 5
♥ K
♦ K J 9 7 5
♣ K J 6

13. Your side is vulnerable and the opponents not. You deal and pass with the following hand:

♠ A Q 6
♥ 6 4
♦ 9 7 5 3
♣ A J 10 6

What do you bid when your partner doubles a one-spade opening and the next opponent passes?

14. Both sides are vulnerable. You are South and hold:

> ♠ –
> ♥ 10 7 5 3 2
> ♦ A K
> ♣ A 8 7 4 3 2

West, as dealer, bids one club and your partner doubles. What do you do when the next player passes?

15. The bidding goes:

South	West	North	East
1 ♠	2 ♥	3 ♠	

Is this bid (a) forcing; (b) encouraging?

16. The bidding goes (neither side vulnerable):

West	North	East	South
Pass	Pass	1 ♣	1 ♦
Pass	3 ♥ or 4 ♦		

What sort of hand does North have?

17. Both sides are vulnerable. You are North and the bidding has gone:

East	South	West	North
4 ♣	4 ♠	5 ♣	5 ♦
6 ♣	6 ♦	Pass	6 ♠
Pass	Pass	7 ♣	?

Your hand is:

> ♠ Q 5 2
> ♥ J 9 5 3
> ♦ A Q J 10 9 8
> ♣ –

(a) Do you agree with five diamonds? If not, what alternative do you prefer?
(b) What do you do now?

18. North and South are vulnerable. The bidding has gone:

South	West	North	East
1 ♠	Pass	2 ♦	Pass
3 ♠	Pass	4 NT	5 ♥
?			

What do you bid with:

♠ A Q J 6 3 2
♥ A K 5
♦ Q J 6
♣ J

19. Both sides are vulnerable. Your left-hand opponent deals and bids one diamond which is passed around to you. What do you bid with:

♠ J 9 6 5 2
♥ K Q 5 3
♦ A Q 8
♣ Q

20. Your opponents are vulnerable and you are not. Your left-hand opponent deals and bids four hearts. What do you do when your partner doubles, your right-hand opponent passes, and you hold:

♠ K 4
♥ 7 6 4
♦ 9 8 4
♣ K J 10 9 8

21. Both sides are vulnerable. You are East and the bidding has gone:

South	West	North	East
1 ♦	1 NT	Pass	Pass
Dbl.	Pass	2 ♦	?

What do you call with:

♠ 10 6 5
♥ Q 8 7 3
♦ A J 4
♣ 10 6 3

22. Your hand is:

♠ 7
♥ A K 10 9 7 3
♦ A 4
♣ K Q 9 8

Your side is vulnerable and the opponents are not. What do you bid as North after the following auction:

South	West	North	East
Pass	1 ♠	Dbl.	Pass
2 NT	4 ♦	?	

23. The opponents only are vulnerable, and you are North in this auction:

West	North	East	South
1 ♦	Pass	Pass	1 ♥
Dbl.	?		

What do you bid with:

♠ J 8 4 2
♥ Q J 8 5
♦ 4 3
♣ A Q 5

24. Your side only is vulnerable, and the bidding starts:

West	North	East	South
Pass	3 ♣	3 ♥	3 ♠
?			

What do you call with:

♠ K 8 2
♥ K
♦ K 10 6 3
♣ Q 9 7 5 4

25. Both sides vulnerable. You deal with this hand:

♠ A K 8 4 3
♥ K
♦ A 9
♣ A 9 6 5 3
SOUTH

The bidding goes:

South	West	North	East
1 ♠	2 ♥	Pass	Pass
3 ♣	3 ♦	3 ♠	Pass
?			

What do you do now?

26. Your partner has opened with a weak two-heart bid, both sides vulnerable. Your right-hand opponent overcalls two spades. What do you bid with:

♠ J 9 6 2
♥ Q 7 4
♦ 7
♣ J 9 8 6 4

27. The bidding goes:

South	West	North	East
1 ♣	1 NT	2 ♥	

Is North's bid (a) forcing; (b) encouraging; (c) discouraging; (d) a command to pass?

28. Opponents are vulnerable and you are North.

West	North	East	South
1 ♦	Pass	Pass	1 ♥
Dbl.	Redbl.	2 ♦	3 ♣
Pass	?		

What do you bid now with:

♠ J 8 4 2
♥ Q J 8 5
♦ 4 3
♣ A Q 5

29. Both sides are vulnerable, and you are South with:

♠ J 10 7
♥ K 9 7 3
♦ K 5 4 2
♣ Q 6

What do you call after the following auction:

East	South	West	North
Pass	Pass	1 ♥	Dbl.
2 ♥	?		

Answers

1. Double, 10 points; one no-trump, 8; pass, 3.
It would be cowardly to pass, but the decision whether to double or bid one no-trump is close. The no-trump overcall promises the strength for a no-trump opening, and you are one point short. Against that, the double suggests slightly more support for the major suits than you have. (See hand 10)

2. One heart or two hearts, 10 points.
Although your suit is on the feeble side, you have a powerful 6-4-2-1 distribution, and your diamond honours should win two tricks. One heart misses the opportunity to crowd the bidding for the opponents, so players who use pre-emptive jump overcalls should bid two hearts. (See hand 19)

3. Two hearts, 10 points; three hearts or four hearts, 3.
At first sight this might seem a good hand for a pre-emptive jump to three hearts or four hearts. But a pre-emptive action may easily goad your partner into sacrificing against four spades, and you do not want him to do that: your spade holding offers good prospects of defeating four spades, and will not be of great value in a heart contract. By bidding two hearts you imply some defensive strength, and it is less likely that your partner will embark on a save. (See hand 20)

4. Four spades, 10 points.
At this vulnerability the strongest possible pre-emptive action is called for. Three spades would be about right at the opposite vulnerability: vulnerable against not. (See hand 31)

5. Three hearts (strong), 10 points; double 8.
Your hand is too strong for a simple overcall of two hearts, and much too weak for a cue bid of two spades. A three heart bid shows a good heart suit and about this strength.

A reasonable alternative is to double and then bid hearts, but most tournament players use this method to show a stronger hand. (See hand 39)

6. Two hearts, 10 points; four no-trumps, 8; two no-trumps, 5; double, 2.
A hand of such great power justifies a cue bid, indicating a determination to reach game. Four no-trumps would be Black-wood and has merit. Two no-trumps would be the 'unusual' no-trump showing the minors, but not in such great strength. A double would wrongly suggest the possession of some spades.
(See hand 21)

7. One spade (or two spades if using weak jump overcalls), 10 points; three spades, 6.
At any other vulnerability a pre-emptive jump to three spades would get the top ranking. But there is too great a danger of losing 500 points or more, when the opposing game is worth only about 400. (See hand 12)

8. Double, 10 points; pass, 5.
Holding only two diamonds the double is not ideal, but the chance that partner will respond one diamond and the opponents will remain silent is not great. This slight risk is worth taking in the interests of finding a major-suit fit. (See hand 23)

9. Double, 10 points; four spades, 6; three spades, 3.
A double is for penalties and shows a powerful hand in high cards. If you get another chance you will bid three spades, a very strong game invitation. A direct four-spade bid is a slight gamble, but not unreasonable. (See hand 15)

10. Two clubs, 10 points; double, 5.
The traditional cue bid of two clubs, showing an enormous hand with game expectations, is entirely suitable. However, since one club can be a three-card suit some players prefer to treat the two-club bid as a natural bid with length in clubs, much the

same as an overcall of another suit. For those who bid this way,
or those who think their partners might hold that opinion, a
take-out double, perhaps followed by a club cue bid on the next
round, meets the case.   (See hand 37)

11. Six spades, 10 points; five diamonds, 9; pass, seven spades, 3.

Your hand should be worth five tricks—two club ruffs and three
aces—so 12 tricks should be attainable. A direct slam bid is
called for, or perhaps a cue bid of five diamonds followed by six
spades. You can expect your partner to have a singleton in one
of the red suits, so the danger of having two unavoidable losers
is not great. Seven spades might just make if partner has a singleton or void heart, but is much too optimistic. Five spades will
not lead anywhere, because partner is virtually sure to pass.

(See hand 31)

12. Double, 10 points; one spade, 5.

The double is, of course, for take-out and implies a three-suited
hand. A bid of one spade would not indicate that you are willing
to play in clubs. If your partner has a five-card club suit he will
not bid it over one spade and you will miss your best spot.

(See hand 47)

13. Two no-trumps, 10 points; two spades, 5.

Two no-trumps describes the hand perfectly: a balanced hand,
about 11 points, and the opponent's suit well-stopped. The
original pass does not affect the meaning of the bid. The cue bid
of two spades shows a maximum pass, but does not indicate the
strong orientation of the hand towards no-trumps. Three clubs
shows the right strength, but places too much emphasis on clubs.

(See hand 39)

14. Two clubs, 10 points; two hearts, 5; four hearts, 2.

With powerful distribution and controls you can afford to insist
on a game. Four hearts is where you expect to land, but there is
no need to prejudge the issue by making that bid at once.

(See hand 37)

15. Encouraging, 10 points.

The three-spade bid is exactly the same limit bid as it would
have been without the intervention of two hearts. Without that

bid it would have shown four-card spade support and in the region of 11–12 points, which is what you still have.

(See hand 20)

16. Four diamonds or three hearts, 10 points.

A 'shape' hand with a massive diamond fit. His excitement over an original pass could be due to nothing else. 'Shape' also implies shortages, which should encourage South to go to game.

Four diamonds is the bid which would be made by most players in Britain, but three hearts is what is known as a 'splinter bid', which is unlikely to be known by any other than users of 'Precision', for which reason both bids gain the maximum award.

(See hand 7)

17. (a) Prefer six clubs, 10 points; prefer six spades, 7; agree with five diamonds, 5; prefer five spades, 3.

You have a very powerful hand when partner has made a vulnerable overcall at the level of four. Six spades looks good, and a grand slam is not out of reach. The cue bid gives the right message.

(b) Pass, 10 points; seven diamonds or seven spades, 7; double, 3.

As we had bid six spades expecting to make it and the opponents are clearly sacrificing, the pass is forcing. It indicates a hand suitable for a grand slam, and permits South to make the final decision.

(See hand 3)

18. Five no-trumps, 10 points; double, 5.

This is perhaps an unfair question, since the answer depends on partnership understanding. One solution is to double for penalties, pass with no ace, make a one-step bid with one ace, and so on. On this basis the answer would be five no-trumps, a two-step bid. The most popular American agreement is to double with no ace, two aces, or four aces, and pass with one or three aces. This makes sure that the overcaller cannot escape if the four no-trump bidder wants to penalise him. This arrangement is known as DOPI (double= 0, pass= 1). The opposite is DOPE (double with odd, pass with even), which is rare but just as good.

(See hand 4)

19. One spade, 10 points; double, 5.

In a protective situation you should bid rather as you would in the direct position but with more freedom. By bidding one spade you have a fair prospect of being able to show hearts later. A take-out double may uncover a major suit fit quickly, but will work badly if North responds two clubs. If South passes he is probably leaving his partner in the wrong contract, and if he bids two spades he will give an impression of greater strength. Some players believe that a protective bid in a suit denies the strength for an opening bid, but this is a fallacy.   (See hand 24)

20. Pass, 10 points; five clubs, 5.

In this situation the double would normally be taken as a business one, and doubtless four hearts will go down a trick or two. Five clubs is a gamble: it may not make against the bad breaks which are certainly in store.   (See hand 17)

21. Double, 10 points; two no-trumps, 6.

If your partner has the hand he has shown, a one no-trump opening bid with something in diamonds, the opponents must be in trouble. Put them in more trouble with a double.

(See hand 10)

22. Four hearts, 10 points.

Four hearts should be your right contract. The penalty to be had from doubling four diamonds will not compensate you for the loss of a vulnerable game.   (See hand 39)

23. Two no-trumps or redouble, 10 points; three hearts, 5; two hearts, 3.

This situation closely resembles the common one in which your partner's opening bid has been doubled. The redouble shows general high-card strength, probably nine or more points. An immediate heart raise would have a pre-emptive flavour, and would suggest less high-card strength.

In Britain the redouble is usually used to show willingness to defend, which loses much of its attraction when one holds a four-card fit for partner. In these circumstances we use a bid of two no-trumps to show full values for a three heart raise. You are on the lightish side for this, for which reason both bids are awarded full marks. (See hand 47)

24. Pass, 10 points.
With a misfit hand there is no reason to think that your side can make anything. There is no guarantee that you can defeat three spades, and in any case the bidding is not going to stop there—three spades is a forcing bid. (See hand 28)

25. Pass, 10 points; four spades, 5.
You have bid your hand very strongly already. You know that bad breaks are likely in the black suits. You also know that your partner must be very weak, for he could not bring himself to bid two spades on the first round. Four spades would get a lower rating in spite of the fact that an optimistic expert chose that bid. (See hand 16)

26. Three hearts, 10 points; four hearts or pass, 5.
The trump support and diamond singleton justify a mild attempt to push the opponents higher. Four hearts would be too aggressive, and a pass too cowardly. (See hand 22)

27. (c) Discouraging, 10 points.
With any hand of moderate strength (say nine points or better) North would double one no-trump. His bid, therefore, suggests a weak hand but a long, strong suit, probably six cards or longer. (See hand 19)

28. Four hearts, 10 points; three hearts, 5.
Your partner's bid of three clubs showed his distribution, but was not particularly encouraging—with a good hand in high cards he would have left the next move to you, relying on your redouble, and shown his distribution later. Nevertheless you have such a good fit, with nine of your high-card points in his suits, that the game should be bid. (See hand 47)

29. Two no-trumps, 10 points; three diamonds, 9; double or two spades, 5.
If a game is to be made, no-trumps is the only hope. Two no-trumps is the only way to head for game. Three diamonds should

produce a safe part-score contract, and may work out better than two no-trumps if the doubler has a minimum hand. A double is not quite appropriate, whether it is intended for penalties or for take-out. (Many tournament players use 'responsive', or take-out, doubles in this position.) An imaginative two-spade bid, assuming that North has a four-card spade suit, has something to recommend it. (See hand 18)

Awards

260–300	OUTSTANDING
200–250	VERY GOOD INDEED
150–190	ABOVE AVERAGE
100–140	BELOW AVERAGE
50–90	FAIR
0–40	POOR

Playing with the Dummy

In this section, divided into three sub-sections, your skill in handling the dummy will be tested—and tested quite severely.

In the first section the right theoretical way to handle some combinations is presented. In some of them there is a practical angle: the ability of the opponents may determine the most effective method of manoeuvring.

In the second and third sections you are presented with a problem in planning the play. In some cases it is necessary to follow the play to the first few tricks to reach the point of decision. In such cases the less experienced reader is advised to write down the position in which the decision must be made, or even to use a pack of cards.

A word of warning—these are tough. Few experts would score 100 per cent, so do not be disappointed if you have a poor score.

Suit Combinations

1. What is the best percentage play to develop four tricks from:

> NORTH
>
> ♦ 3
>
> SOUTH
>
> ♦ A J 10 6 5 2

2. Consider this suit combination:

> NORTH
>
> ♦ A K 9
>
> SOUTH
>
> ♦ J 6 5 3 2

(a) How do you play for four tricks?
(b) How do you play for five tricks?

3. Consider this combination:

> NORTH
>
> ♠ K Q 10
>
> SOUTH
>
> ♠ 5 4 3

You lead low to the king or queen, and it wins. Later you lead low again, and a low card is played to your left What do you play?

4.
> NORTH
>
> ♥ A 8 4 3
>
> SOUTH
>
> ♥ K Q 10 2

(a) How should you play if East drops the nine under your king?
(b) Does it matter which hand leads to the first trick?

5. Late in the play you force your left-hand opponent to open up a suit in which you can see:

NORTH

♦ K 9 6 3

SOUTH

♦ A 10 4

(a) How would you play if he leads an honour?
(b) Would your answer be different if West is an expert?
(c) How would you play if West leads a low card?
(d) Would your answer be different if West is an expert?

Answers

---

1. Play the diamond ace followed by a low card, 10 points; take a first-round finesse, 3.
If the suit splits three-three any play wins, and the same is true if the right-hand opponent has a doubleton honour. But if there is a doubleton on the left it is more likely to include one honour (eight cases) than no honour (six cases). The second choice is an immediate finesse, which works against a small doubleton on the left. The play of the ace followed by an honour has nothing to recommend it whatsoever.   (See hand 13)

2. (a) Play a top diamond, then return to the South hand in another suit and lead to the nine, 10 points.
This guarantees four tricks unless the suit is divided 5-0.
    (b) Play the ace and king, 10 points.
You must hope for the queen to fall doubleton. But if it falls from your right-hand opponent on the first trick, finesse the nine later.   (See hand 36)

3. Play for the stronger opponent to have the ace, 10 points.
This is a guess on the face of it: which way round are the ace and jack? But a weak defender is liable to have played the ace by this time, whereas a strong player will duck without any revealing hesitation sitting on either side of the table.   (See hand 27)

4. (a) The answer depends on the ability of your opponents. Against experts, assume that East has falsecarded with ♥ J 9 x x and lead to dummy's ace. Against less-than-experts, assume the nine is a singleton and play the queen to the second trick, **10 points**—hard-earned.

(b) Yes. It is slightly better to lead a low heart from dummy on the first-trick, because it is then harder for East to falsecard with J 9 x x, **10 points.**   (See hand 46)

5. (a) If an honour is led by a weak or average player, you should assume he has the other honour and play low from dummy, **10 points.**

(b) If the honour is led by an expert, assume he does not have the other honour and play dummy's king, **10 points.**

(c) If a low card is led, you normally assume that the leader has one honour. Play low from dummy, **10 points.**

(d) However, if a low card is led by an expert—who would lead an honour if he could—your best chance may be to assume that the other defender has both missing honours doubleton, **10 points.**   (See hand 48)

Awards

80–100	OUTSTANDING
50–70	VERY GOOD INDEED
20–40	FAIR
0–10	POOR

Part Scores and Games

1. You reach four hearts against silent opponents with the following:

NORTH
♠ Q 10 5 4
♥ A 10 9
♦ 6
♣ K J 10 7 2

SOUTH
♠ K 8 7
♥ K Q 6 5 4 2
♦ K Q
♣ 6 5

The diamond five is led and won with the ace by East, who returns a trump. Plan the play.

2. Your hands are:

NORTH
♠ J 8 6 2
♥ 5
♦ J 9 5 4 3
♣ A K 10

SOUTH
♠ 10
♥ A Q J 7 6 3 2
♦ A Q 7
♣ J 6

The opponents are vulnerable, and you reach four hearts. West has bid two spades (weak) over one heart and led the spade king. East follows with the five, and West switches to the club two. Plan the play to this trick and the subsequent trick.

3. You reach four hearts against silent opponents after your partner has opened in fourth seat with one diamond.

> NORTH
> ♠ Q 4
> ♥ A Q J 3
> ♦ A 8 6 2
> ♣ J 7 5
>
> SOUTH
> ♠ K 7
> ♥ 10 9 7 6 4 2
> ♦ K J 10 3
> ♣ 8

West leads the spade ace followed by the club ace and the club four. East contributes the spade three, the club nine and the club queen. You ruff. What now?

4. You reach three no-trumps, optimistically, after your partner's third-seat one-club bid has been doubled on your right. You can see:

> NORTH
> ♠ Q J 10 2
> ♥ A 4
> ♦ Q J
> ♣ A J 7 5 2
>
> SOUTH
> ♠ A 8
> ♥ J 7 5
> ♦ A 8 6 5 4 2
> ♣ 10 3

The heart two is led, and East wins with the queen. He returns the three to dummy's ace. What is your plan?

5. You bid four spades directly over an opening bid on your right of one no-trump, showing 16–18 points.

NORTH
♠ J 5
♥ J 8 7 2
♦ 10 9 6 2
♣ 8 4 3

SOUTH
♠ A Q 10 9 8 7
♥ A
♦ A K J 4
♣ 6 5

West leads the club queen, which wins. The club seven is continued and East plays the king followed by the ace. Plan the play.

6. You reach three no-trumps after the following auction:

East	South	West	North
Pass	Pass	1 ♥	Dbl.
2 ♥	2 NT	Pass	3 NT
Pass	Pass	Pass	

Plan the play after the lead of the diamond nine with the following hands:

NORTH
♠ A K 9 3
♥ 2
♦ A Q 8 6
♣ J 10 5 3

SOUTH
♠ J 10 7
♥ K 9 7 3
♦ K 5 4 2
♣ Q 6

7. You reach three no-trumps and the opening lead is the spade eight (the unbid suit). Plan the play with:

NORTH
♠ K 6 3
♥ A 9 8 4
♦ 3
♣ A J 8 4 2

SOUTH
♠ A J 5
♥ J 10
♦ A J 10 6 5 2
♣ 5 3

8. You open one spade and your partner raises to four spades after an overcall of two hearts.

NORTH
♠ 9 7 6 3
♥ Q
♦ J 8 4
♣ A K 9 4 3

SOUTH
♠ A 10 5 4 2
♥ A 2
♦ A 7 6 3
♣ 10 8

(a) Plan your play after the opening lead of the spade king.
(b) How do you expect the trumps to be divided?

9. Both sides are vulnerable. The bidding was:

South	West	North	East
1 ♠	2 ♥	Pass	Pass
3 ♣	3 ♦	3 ♠	Pass
4 ♠	Pass	Pass	Pass

NORTH
♠ 9 7 2
♥ Q 9 6
♦ 10 7
♣ Q J 10 7 2

SOUTH
♠ A K 8 4 3
♥ K
♦ A 9
♣ A 9 6 5 3

Plan the play after the opening lead of the diamond king. What construction of the opponents' hands will give you a chance to make the contract?

10. Your hands are:

NORTH
♠ A 10 6
♥ K Q 8 7 3
♦ A
♣ 10 8 5 4

SOUTH
♠ K Q J 9 5 4 3
♥ J
♦ Q 7 2
♣ K 3

You reach a precarious contract of five spades after your partner has opened one heart and your right-hand opponent has overcalled two clubs. Plan the play after the opening lead of the club queen.

11. After an opening bid of one diamond on your left, and no further opposition bidding, you reach four spades with:

NORTH

♠ A 7 4
♥ A 9 8 7
♦ 5 3
♣ J 9 7 2

SOUTH

♠ J 9 6 5 2
♥ K Q 5 3
♦ A Q 8
♣ Q

West leads the club king and switches to the spade king, which you permit to win. He switches to the heart four, and you take East's ten with the king. What next?

12. East-West are vulnerable, you are South, and the bidding has gone:

West	North	East	South
1 ♦	Pass	Pass	1 ♥
Dbl.	Redbl.	2 ♦	3 ♣
Pass	4 ♥	Pass	Pass
Pass			

NORTH

♠ J 8 4 2
♥ Q J 8 5
♦ 4 3
♣ A Q 5

SOUTH

♠ Q 7
♥ A 10 9 7 6
♦ A
♣ 9 8 7 4 3

West leads the spade king.

(a) Plan the play if West switches to the diamond seven and East plays the queen.

(b) Plan the play if West switches to the diamond king.

(c) Would your plans be affected if you knew that West was a top-ranking expert?

13. Your hands are:

> NORTH
> ♠ A 9 7 6 3 2
> ♥ K 8 7
> ♦ A Q
> ♣ Q 5
>
> SOUTH
> ♠ J 10
> ♥ -
> ♦ K J 10 6 3
> ♣ A K J 10 7 6

The bidding was:

West	North	East	South
Pass	1 ♠	Pass	2 ♣
Pass	2 NT	Pass	3 ♦
Pass	3 ♠	Pass	4 ♦
Pass	5 ♦	Dbl.	Redbl.
Pass	Pass	Pass	

Plan the play after the opening lead of the heart ten.

14. You overcalled one club by East with one diamond. Your partner jumps to four diamonds which you raise to game.
So you are playing five diamonds with the following cards:

> NORTH
> ♠ J 10 5 3
> ♥ 10
> ♦ A Q J 9
> ♣ Q J 8 5
>
> SOUTH
> ♠ A 6
> ♥ Q 6 5 4
> ♦ K 10 8 6 3
> ♣ A 3

The club ten is led, and the jack wins in dummy. A heart lead is won by East with the king, and he leads a low club. South wins with the ace, ruffs a heart, leads to the spade ace and ruffs another heart. Plan the play.

15. Against silent opponents you reach four hearts after opening one heart in third seat.

NORTH
♠ 9 5 3
♥ 10 9 4 2
♦ K 9 6 3
♣ 7 4

SOUTH
♠ K J 7 2
♥ A K 8 6 3
♦ A 10 4
♣ A

The club five is led to East's queen and your ace. You play two top trumps, and East has a small singleton. You give West his trump trick, and he plays the club three to East's king. East has discarded the two and six of clubs. Plan the play at this point.

16. You reach a slightly optimistic three no-trumps contract, with the opponents silent. You can see:

NORTH
♠ J 5 2
♥ 10 7 5
♦ K 8 7
♣ A 10 7 6

SOUTH
♠ Q 7 6
♥ A Q J
♦ A 6 5 4 2
♣ K 3

West leads the spade nine. You play low from dummy, East plays the three, and you win with the queen. Plan the play.

17. You reach four hearts after your left-hand opponent has overcalled non-vulnerable with one spade.

NORTH
♠ Q 8 2
♥ K 7 6 3
♦ 8 6 2
♣ A J 4

SOUTH
♠ 7
♥ A Q J 10 9 8
♦ A Q 4
♣ K 5 2

West leads the spade king and switches to the club ten.
(a) Plan your play.
(b) Plan your play if you have optimistically reached six hearts.

18. You can see:

NORTH
♠ Q 8
♥ A J 9 8 4
♦ Q 10 3 2
♣ J 5

SOUTH
♠ K J 10 7 6 5 2
♥ Q 10 3
♦ –
♣ Q 8 2

Neither side is vulnerable, and you play four spades doubled after a complex auction:

East	South	West	North
1 ♦	1 ♠	2 ♣	2 ♥
Pass	2 ♠	3 ♣	Pass
Pass	3 ♥	Pass	3 ♠
Pass	4 ♠	Dbl.	Pass
Pass	Pass		

West leads the diamond four. You play the diamond ten from dummy and East plays the ace which you ruff.

(a) Analyse the bidding and play so far to determine as closely as you can the distribution of high cards in the defenders' hands.

(b) Decide your next play.

Answers

1. Win with ♥ K or ♥ Q and lead a club to dummy's ♣ J or ♣ 10, 10 points; win with ♥ K or ♥ Q and lead a club to dummy's ♣ K, 5 points. Deduct 2 points for playing two rounds of trumps before attacking clubs.

If the club jack wins or forces the ace—proving that West has the queen—you are home regardless of the spade situation. Any other play offers lesser chances. (See hand 26)

2. The club two may well be a singleton so you must try to prevent a club ruff. Win in dummy and finesse in hearts hoping that West does not have a singleton heart king, 10 points.

As West is unlikely to have any strength outside spades, this is a lesser risk than the apparent safety play of the heart ace followed by the queen. (See hand 12)

3. Lead to the heart ace, 10 points.

West passed originally and has produced two aces. He is unlikely to have the heart king, and if he does have that card the diamond queen will be marked in the East hand. The declarer gives himself the chance of finding the singleton heart king on his right. (See hand 6)

4. Lead a diamond honour from dummy and play low, whether or not East plays the king, 10 points.

There is a fair chance of making five diamond tricks, two spades and two aces, but care is needed. If the queen is covered by the king you have no chance if you take with the ace. By playing low on the diamond you will succeed if the diamonds are three-two and the defenders do not attack your spade entry.

(See hand 23)

5. Ruff and lead the spade queen. If this wins lead the diamond jack, 10 points.

East must have both the spade king and the diamond queen to justify his bidding. A four-one break in either suit will be fatal, so we assume three-two. The recommended play forces East to surrender a potential trick or to allow declarer access to dummy in one suit to finesse in the other. (See hand 15)

6. Take a spade finesse and if it wins run all possible winners in spades and diamonds.

This will make it harder in the end-game for the defence to take the five tricks that are probably due to them: three hearts and two clubs. Eventually play clubs and hope for the best, **10 points.** (See hand 18)

7. Win with the spade king, 10 points; then lead a diamond to the ace followed by a small diamond, 5 more points.

You need two spade entries in your hand to develop and use the diamonds. The lead strongly suggests that East has the spade queen so you must win the first trick in dummy and play diamonds. The diamond ace followed by a small card is the percentage play, for the left-hand opponent is more likely to have a doubleton honour than a small doubleton. (See hand 13)

8. (a) Duck the opening lead, and plan to develop clubs as quickly as possible, 10 points.

The duck in trumps helps to keep control. The best chance of making the contract is to find a three-three club division.

(b) The opening leader almost certainly has king-queen-jack of trumps.

With any other holding (king, king-queen, king-queen-jack-x) he would jeopardise a trick by leading the suit. (Take **5 bonus points** for working this out correctly.) (See hand 20)

9. Allow the diamond king to win, 10 points. If West then cashes the heart ace and plays another diamond, play ace and a low trump, 10 more points.

West's bidding indicates 11 cards in the red suits. He must have two spades for us to have a chance, therefore we assume a void club. East must not be given the chance to give his partner a club ruff, and we must find a way to reach the dummy eventually for a club finesse. If West has a doubleton spade queen and fails to play the honour under the ace ...   (See hand 16)

10. Drop the club king when East plays the ace, 10 points.
It is highly unlikely that East has overcalled with a broken five-card suit. If he has six you are about to run into an immediate ruff. Your best chance is to persuade him that you have a single-ton, with a long-term chance of discarding your remaining club on dummy's hearts.   (See hand 40)

11. Lead to the spade ace and play the heart eight, planning a finesse, 10 points.
West has bid diamonds, and can be assumed to have king-queen-ten of spades and the ace-king of clubs. He was reluctant to lead another club, so the chances are that he has nothing in hearts. The finesse should be taken against East to preserve the ace as a later entry to the dummy.   (See hand 24)

12. (a) Play the heart ace, 10 points.
As East has the diamond queen and diamond support, he is most unlikely to have the heart king, for he would have raised one diamond to two diamonds. There is a fair chance that West has a singleton heart king.
  (b) Take a club finesse and then a heart finesse, 10 points.
West probably has a heart singleton, and there is no reason to think it is the king.
  (c) Play the heart ace in both situations, 10 points.
West is liable to be falsecarding with the diamond king to encourage you to finesse in hearts. If he held a small singleton heart and the king-queen of diamonds, he would probably lead the diamond queen to make you think East has the diamond king.   (See hand 47)

13. Play low from dummy, ruff, cross to the diamond ace, and lead clubs, 10 points.
East can be presumed to have length in diamonds for his double, and we must hope not more than five of them. The second round of trumps must not be taken because it is needed as an entry to

the closed hand later. You ruff the first heart rather than the second in order to keep a guard for dummy's king.

(See hand 8)

14. Lead a spade, 20 points.

Whatever the defence does, South can continue his cross-ruff. But if he cross-ruffs at once, ruffing clubs high to avoid a possible overruff, West is liable eventually to take a trick with the diamond seven. That card may be promoted if East wins a late trick in spades and plays yet another club. (See hand 7)

15. Ruff the club king and lead a low spade, aiming for an end play, 20 points.

East apparently began with five clubs headed by the king-queen and a singleton heart. If in addition he held ace-queen of spades he would probably have opened the bidding. The best chance, a hard one to see, is to play West for a doubleton spade ace. If this is the situation, the lead of a low spade at this point, followed by another low spade when there is an opportunity, will force West to open up diamonds or concede a ruff and discard.

(See hand 48)

16. Lead a spade, 20 points.

To have any chance the heart finesse must win, so you assume that. This will give you eight tricks. The best chance of the ninth is to develop a squeeze, so you must let West take his spade tricks. If West had only four spades originally you can still develop the diamonds. If West had five spades he can take four tricks but you have good chances of squeezing your right-hand opponent in the minor suits. If it turns out that West started life with six spades you will have to shoot yourself, but your survival prospects are pretty good. (See hand 11)

17. (a) Allow the club ten to win, 20 points.

You can then make when both minor suit finesses lose: at the right moment, after drawing trumps, ruffing one spade and cashing the king and ace of clubs, you can play the spade queen from dummy and discard a diamond to endplay West.

(b) Play the club jack from dummy, 20 points.

You must assume that both minor-suit finesses will win, and also that West has five diamonds, not including the king. In that case he can be squeezed in spades and diamonds by leading all the trumps, followed by two club winners, ending in dummy.

(See hand 14)

18. (a) West must have the diamond king, the ace or king of clubs, but not both, and either the spade ace or the heart king, 20 points.

East's play of the diamond ace (unless he has made an unlikely falsecard) shows that West has the diamond king. West has bid and rebid clubs, suggesting a six-card suit. He would have led an ace-king holding, so he must have one top club but not both.

The bidding showed that East has about 12 points and West about 10, a total that meshes with the 18 high-card points in the North-South hands. To make up his point-count West must have the spade ace or the heart king, but not both. We must assume the heart king to have any prospects of making the contract.

(b) Lead a club, 20 points.

If the heart king is on-side, it seems easy to make ten tricks. But there is a lurking danger. As the clubs are probably split six-two, East may make the spade nine on the third round of clubs.

If at any time the defenders play the third round of clubs, we want to be in a position to ruff with the spade queen. Leading to the spade queen is, therefore, wrong, and so is a trump honour lead from the closed hand—East can then duck with ♠ A 9 x. A club play cuts the defenders' communications, but is not easy to see. (See hand 43)

Awards

250–300	OUTSTANDING
200–240	VERY GOOD INDEED
150–190	ABOVE AVERAGE
100–140	BELOW AVERAGE
50–90	FAIR
0–40	POOR

Slams

1. You bid quickly to six no-trumps against silent opponents.

NORTH

♠ 6 4

♥ A K 7 3

♦ A 10 6

♣ A Q 7 2

SOUTH

♠ A Q 7 2

♥ Q 5 2

♦ Q J 5

♣ K J 5

The opening lead is the heart jack.

Is the slam: (a) a sound contract? (b) an unsound contract? (c) a borderline proposition?

2. Against silent opponents you reach seven no-trumps holding:

NORTH

♠ A K Q

♥ A 4

♦ K J 8 5 3

♣ K Q J

SOUTH

♠ 9 4 2

♥ K Q 7

♦ A 10 4 2

♣ A 5 2

Plan the play after the opening lead of the spade jack.

3. You reach six diamonds against silent opponents, and your hands are:

NORTH

♠ J
♥ A 4 2
♦ A K 7 4
♣ A K Q 9 8

SOUTH

♠ K 7 5 3
♥ K J 6 5
♦ Q J 8 3
♣ 3

West leads the spade ace and continues with the eight. Plan your play.

4. Against silent opponents you reach six spades with:

NORTH

♠ 4 2
♥ A K Q 10 9 6
♦ -
♣ A K Q 4 3

SOUTH

♠ A K Q 8 7
♥ 7
♦ K 10 6 3 2
♣ J 2

Plan the play after the opening lead of the spade jack.

5. You reach six clubs doubled after the following auction:

SOUTH	WEST	NORTH	EAST
Pass	1 ♠	Dbl.	Pass
2 NT	4 ♦	Dbl.	4 ♠
4 NT	Pass	5 ♥	Dbl.
Pass	Pass	5 NT	Dbl.
6 ♣	Pass	Pass	Dbl.
Pass	Pass	Pass	

NORTH
♠ 7
♥ A K 10 9 7 3
♦ A 4
♣ K Q 9 8

SOUTH
♠ A Q 6
♥ 6 4
♦ 9 7 5 3
♣ A J 10 6

Plan the play after the opening lead of the diamond king.

6. You overcall one diamond with four spades (opponents vulnerable) and your partner raises you to six spades. Your hands are:

NORTH
♠ A 4 3 2
♥ A 10 5 4 3 2
♦ A 5 4
♣ -

SOUTH
♠ K J 10 9 8 7 6 5
♥ K
♦ J 7 6 3
♣ -

West leads the diamond two. Plan the play.

7. Against silent opponents you reach six no-trumps with the following:

NORTH
♠ Q 8
♥ A J
♦ K 6 2
♣ A K Q 9 7 5

SOUTH
♠ K J 5
♥ K Q 10
♦ A 9 8 7 3
♣ 10 2

West leads the spade three and East takes the ace. The ten is returned, and West follows with the two. Plan the play.

8. You reach six no-trumps with:

NORTH
♠ Q 3
♥ K Q
♦ 8 7 3
♣ A J 10 5 4 3

SOUTH
♠ A 10 4
♥ A 8 4 3
♦ K Q 9
♣ K Q 9

West has doubled six no-trumps, and also an earlier conventional bid of five spades by you. He leads the club six, and you win with the ten in dummy. You lead a diamond to the king, and West takes the ace and plays the club seven. Plan your play.

9. Against silent opponents you reach six spades with these hands:

NORTH
♠ Q 6 4 2
♥ A Q J
♦ 7 3
♣ 9 7 6 5

SOUTH
♠ A K 8 5 3
♥ 7
♦ A K 8 4
♣ A Q 4

Plan the play after the opening lead of the spade jack, on which East will play the seven.

10. You reach six spades against silent opponents, holding the following hands:

NORTH
♠ Q J 4
♥ K Q 9 8 3
♦ J
♣ 9 8 4 2

SOUTH
♠ K 10 9 6 5
♥ -
♦ A K 7 5
♣ A K Q 6

West leads the club seven which is covered by the eight, ten and king. Plan the play.

11. Against silent opponents you reach six no-trumps with the following:

> NORTH
> ♠ 7 4
> ♥ J 2
> ♦ A 10 9
> ♣ A K Q 9 7 3
>
> SOUTH
> ♠ K J 3
> ♥ A K 7 6 5
> ♦ K Q
> ♣ J 10 4

The eight of diamonds is led. Plan the play.

12. You are South, playing seven clubs against silent opponents.

> NORTH
> ♠ A 9 8 6 2
> ♥ K 8 5
> ♦ A
> ♣ A 10 9 2
>
> SOUTH
> ♠ K Q 5
> ♥ A 9 4
> ♦ 9 4 2
> ♣ K Q J 7

Plan the play after the lead of the diamond king.

13. You reach six clubs after the following auction:

North	East	South	West
Pass	Pass	1 ♣	Pass
2 ♦	2 ♥	2 ♠	Pass
4 ♣	Pass	4 NT	Pass
5 ♦	Pass	6 ♣	Pass
Pass	Pass		

NORTH
♠ 7
♥ Q 3
♦ A K 10 7 2
♣ 9 8 7 6 3

SOUTH
♠ A Q 8 5
♥ J
♦ Q 9 3
♣ A Q J 10 5

The lead is the heart five, and East plays the king followed by the ace.
(a) Plan the play.
(b) Would your plan be any different if you knew that East held the spade king? If so why?

14. You are South, and reach seven hearts after West has opened one club.

NORTH
♠ A Q 8
♥ A K Q J
♦ Q J 10 9 8 2
♣ -

SOUTH
♠ -
♥ 10 7 5 3 2
♦ A K
♣ A 8 7 4 3 2

Plan the play after the opening lead of the club king.

15. Against silent opponents you reach seven hearts with these hands:

NORTH
♠ 9 5
♥ A 8 4 3
♦ A Q 7 5
♣ A K 8

SOUTH
♠ A K Q 7 2
♥ K Q 10 2
♦ K 10
♣ J 3

Plan the play after the opening lead of the diamond jack.

16. You pass a hand that most players would open, and a curious auction develops:

East	South	West	North
Pass	Pass	3 ♦	4 ♦
5 ♦	6 N T	Pass	Pass
Dbl.	Redbl.	Pass	Pass
Pass			

NORTH
♠ A 8 7 4 2
♥ A Q 10 7 3
♦ A 5
♣ A

SOUTH
♠ K 3
♥ K 8 6
♦ K Q 2
♣ Q 9 7 6 3

Plan the play against the opening lead of the club jack.

Answers

1. (c) Borderline, 10 points.
You have 10 sure tricks, assuming two in diamonds and the others may come from spades, hearts, and diamonds. A slam that needs two finesses out of three is a 50 per cent chance, and is borderline. Here the fact that the chance of a heart trick is worse than a finesse is balanced by the extra chance of an eventual throw-in play in hearts. (See hand 42)

2. Postpone the diamond guess as long as possible.
Leading out winners in spades, hearts and clubs may provide clues to the distribution which will help you guess the location of the diamond queen, **10 points.** (See hand 29)

3. Discard a heart from dummy and win with the spade king.
Lead to the club ace and ruff a low club with a low trump. Cash the diamond queen and lead a low diamond to dummy's king. If the trumps break, ruff dummy's remaining low club with the diamond jack. If trumps do not break, draw the missing trumps and hope for an even club break or a winning heart finesse, **10 points.** (See hand 30)

4. Allow the spade jack to win, 10 points.
This allows you to keep control against the likely four-two spade division. A trump remains in dummy to deal with a diamond switch, and the declarer should have no trouble in making 12 tricks barring a very bad trump split. (See hand 34)

5. Win with the diamond ace, lead to the spade ace and play the spade queen.
When West covers with the king, discard dummy's diamond loser in the interests of cutting the defenders' communications.

If, as seems likely from the bidding, West has no trumps to lead, you will be able to make the slam by eventually cross-ruffing, making all eight trumps separately, **10 points.**   (See hand 39)

6. Win with the diamond ace, cross to the heart king and lead a low trump, allowing West to win if he produces the queen, 10 points.

West is marked by the bidding and lead with a singleton diamond, so he will have to play a club or a heart, giving South an extra entry to the dummy. This needs a three-three heart break. If West has exactly ♥ Q J x the hand can be made by taking the diamond ace, the heart king, the spade ace, and discarding on a heart lead. Take **3 points** for this line of play, which would be the only chance if West proved to be void when the trump was led towards dummy.   (See hand 31)

7. Test the red suits before playing clubs, 10 points.

The slam is easy if the clubs break normally, so you should probe a little before committing yourself in that suit. Testing the red suits may give you a clue as to the club distribution.
     (See hand 33

8. Win the club in your hand and cash the king-queen of hearts. Take the spade ace and the heart ace, followed by clubs, 10 points.

It is certain from the bidding that West has the spade king, and probable that East is long in hearts, so you will probably execute a double squeeze with diamonds as the pivot suit.
     (See hand 41)

9. Take the queen of spades followed by the ace or king. If West still has a trump take a simple heart finesse. If East still has a trump, take a ruffing finesse in hearts, 10 points.

The player who holds the last trump must not be given the chance to lead it.   (See hand 35

10. Cash the diamond ace and ruff a low diamond at the second trick.

Lead the heart king from dummy, playing East for the ace. If he covers with the ace, ruff and lead a small spade from your hand, **10 points.**   (See hand 1)

11. Win the diamond lead, cross to dummy with a club lead, play a spade and guess. If there are no clues, play for the stronger opponent to have the ace, 10 points.

You cannot afford to delay the spade play. If the player on your right is weak he may put up his ace or think when you lead the suit. If the player on your left is strong, he might make a clever duck when you lead to the king. However you guess, make up your mind before playing from dummy. If your spade play loses, and you have not hesitated about it, your left-hand opponent may not realise the need to return a spade, in which case you have a squeeze chance. (See hand 27)

12. Take the diamond ace, cash the club ace, and lead to the club king.

Ruff a diamond, lead to the heart ace and ruff another diamond. Enter the closed hand with a spade lead and draw trumps. This play guards against a four-one division in one (but not both) of the black suits, **10 points.** (See hand 9)

13. (a) Ruff the second heart lead, cash the spade ace and ruff a spade. Unless the spade king appears, cross to the diamond queen and ruff another spade, 10 points.

If East turns up with the spade king he cannot have the club king, since he passed originally and has shown ace-king of hearts. If you can infer that West has the club king, you must hope it is a singleton and play for the drop.

(b) Play the club ace at once, 5 points.

If you knew that East held the spade king, you would know at once, from East's failure to open the bidding, that West held the club king. (See hand 5)

14. Discard a diamond (not a spade) and play to ruff two spades in the closed hand.

Provided East does not ruff the opening club lead, this play guarantees 13 tricks against virtually any distribution, **10 points.** (See hand 37)

15. Win with the diamond king, enter dummy with a club lead, and play a small heart, 10 points.

This is a very delicate point, based on the possibility that a defender will falsecard the nine from J 9 x x to give you a guess on the second-round of the suit. This falsecard is slightly risky for East if the first trump lead is made from the dummy.

(See hand 46)

16. Win the club ace, cash the ace or queen of hearts, lead to the heart king and continue hearts, 10 points.
There are eleven tricks in sight and no routine way to develop a twelfth. Cashing hearts may embarrass the opponents.

(See hand 38)

Awards

160–200	OUTSTANDING
120–150	VERY GOOD INDEED
80–110	AVERAGE
40–70	FAIR
0–30	POOR

Playing Against
the Dummy

Defence is often considered the hardest part of a game that is seldom easy. Here you can test yourself on opening leads, which means that you must study the auction carefully and draw any deductions you can about the nature of the other three hands. And finally you must solve defensive problems of a challenging character.

If you have worked conscientiously through the previous quizzes you should by now be a sharp analyst. Perhaps you can end up with a good score.

If you are dissatisfied with your scores, read the second section of the book and then put it aside. In a few weeks time, when memory will play a negligible part, attempt the quizzes again. If your scores improve noticeably, you can be satisfied that your hard work has improved both your judgment and your powers of analysis.

Opening Leads

1. You overcall dealer's opening spade bid with two hearts, and your left-hand opponent bids four spades. What do you lead with:

♠ K Q J
♥ K J 10 9 8 7 3
♦ 10
♣ Q 6

2. The opponents have bid one no-trump (strong)—two no-trumps— three no-trumps. What do you lead with:

♠ A K 10 9 4
♥ 8 3 2
♦ 3
♣ 9 8 4 2

3. The bidding has been:

East	South	West	North
Pass	Pass	1 ♥	Dbl.
2 ♥	2 NT	Pass	3 NT
Pass	Pass	Pass	

What do you lead as West with:

♠ Q 6 5
♥ A Q J 8
♦ 9 7 3
♣ A 9 4

4. The bidding has been:

East	South	West	North
1 ♥	3 ♦ (strong)	3 ♥	Pass
Pass	4 ♣	Pass	4 ♥
Pass	6 ♣	Pass	Pass
Pass			

What do you lead as West with:

♠ A Q 10 8 3
♥ 10 7 3
♦ 9 7 2
♣ Q 4

5. Your right-hand opponent opened one no-trump (strong) and was raised to six no-trumps. What do you lead with:

♠ A 9 5 2
♥ 10 4
♦ 8 7 6 3
♣ 8 6 2

6. The bidding has gone:

East	South	West	North
1 ♦	2 ♥*	2 NT	3 ♥
Pass	4 ♥	Dbl.	Pass
Pass	Pass		

* Pre-emptive jump overcall.

What do you lead as West with:

♠ K 5 3
♥ A Q 6
♦ 6 5 4
♣ J 7 4 2

7. The bidding (both confused and confusing) has been:

South	West	North	East
1 ♠	Pass	2 ♦	Pass
3 ♠	Pass	4 NT	5 ♥
5 NT	Pass	6 ♣	Pass
6 ♦	Pass	7 ♠	Pass
Pass	Pass		

What do you lead as West with:

♠ 8 5
♥ J 10 3
♦ 10 8 5 4
♣ 8 4 3 2

8. The bidding was:

South	West	North	East
1 ♦	1 NT	Pass	Pass
Dbl.	Pass	2 ♦	Dbl.
Pass	Pass	Pass	

What do you lead as West with:

♠ K Q 3
♥ A J 2
♦ Q 9 2
♣ K 9 7 2

9. You are West and the bidding has been:

East	South	West	North
4 ♣	4 ♠	5 ♣	5 ♦
6 ♣	6 ♦	Pass	6 ♠
Pass	Pass	7 ♣	Pass
Pass	7 ♠	Pass	Pass
Pass			

What do you lead with:

♠ 9 4
♥ K Q 8 6 4 2
♦ 6 5 4
♣ K 10

10. As West, you listen to the following dialogue by the opponents, who are using strong two-bids.

North	South
2 ♥	2 ♠
3 ♣	3 ♦
3 ♥	3 ♠
5 ♠	6 ♠
Pass	

What do you lead with:

♠ J 10 9 3
♥ J 3 2
♦ A Q 9 8 4
♣ 6

Answers

1. Spade king (or queen or jack), 10 points.
The trump lead should be automatic. Drawing dummy's trumps is likely to be an advantage, and anything else may give away a trick. To play for a ruff would be stupid, because your trumps are sure tricks in any event. (See hand 20)

2. The spade nine (or the ten), 10 points; the spade ace or king, 3.
It is important to provide for the chance that partner has a doubleton spade. If he has a doubleton queen, the lead of a high honour will probably block the suit. If he has a small doubleton, we must lose a trick at once to preserve our communications: we hope he will gain the lead and return his other spade. The unorthodox lead of the four will lose when dummy has a doubleton honour and partner a small doubleton. (See hand 11)

3. A diamond, 10 points; a low club or a low spade, 5.
South surely has the heart king, so a heart lead will give him a vital trick. The passive diamond lead is less likely to give away a trick than a lead in one of the black suits. (See hand 18)

4. Spade ace, 10 points; a heart, 3.
The declarer has a freakish two-suit hand, so you had better try to cash the spade ace at once. If not you may never make it. Also, if you can win the first trick you will have a chance to judge the best defence after seeing dummy. (See hand 21)

5. Any diamond, 10 points; any club, 7; a heart, 4.
With the opponents apparently having balanced hands the first consideration is safety: do not give them any help. A spade lead is, therefore, the worst, and a heart lead the next worst. A club

lead, from a three-card suit, is slightly more likely to trap an honour in partner's hand than a diamond lead from a four-card suit.   (See hand 27)

6. Club two, 10 points; spade three, 8; any diamond, 6.
The diamond is the obvious lead, but that must be what South wants. He has continued optimistically to game when it is obvious to everyone that he is outgunned in high cards. His only justification must be diamond strength which has improved in value because of East's bid. As between the black suits, the club is slightly less likely to give away a trick than the spade.

(See hand 19)

7. A diamond, 10 points; a heart, 8; a club or a spade, 3.
A trump is pointless, and a club can be ruled out: partner would have doubled six clubs if he had wanted that suit led. Which red suit to lead is close. It is improbable that North-South have bid a grand slam without first-round control in East's suit. Against that, East might have doubled seven spades to ask for a lead of dummy's diamond suit if he has the ace. (The confused auction makes it possible that the opponents are missing an ace.)

(See hand 4)

8. Two of diamonds, 10 points; spade king or club two, 5.
The dummy will be very weak, and it is important to cut down ruffs. Partner probably has a diamond honour to justify his double, so the chance of losing a trick by leading from the diamond queen is slight. Anyway, all other leads run a risk of losing a trick.   (See hand 10)

9. Heart king or queen, 10 points; a low heart, 9; a club, 5; a diamond, 3.
This is a tough decision which depends partly on the style of Lightner doubles being used by a partnership. The standard American view is that the double suggests the lead of dummy's suit (rather than any unusual lead) so partner's failure to double rules out the chance that he has a diamond void. But he may have a heart void: his six-club bid suggests that he has some asset apart from the long, strong club suit. This chance seems better than the chance that the opponents have bid a grand slam with an immediate loser in our suit.   (See hand 3)

10. Spade jack (or ten or nine), 10 points; club six, 5.
The trump lead will give nothing away, and will reduce South's chances of ruffing diamonds in the dummy. The club lead gets second rating not so much because it may lead to a ruff—you do not need it—but because it is less likely to give away a trick than a red suit lead.   (See hand 34)

Awards

80–100	OUTSTANDING
50–70	VERY GOOD INDEED
20–40	FAIR
0–10	POOR

Defence Problems

1. The bidding goes:

East	South	West	North
1 ♦	2 ♥ (weak)	2 NT	3 ♥
Pass	4 ♥	Dbl.	Pass
Pass	Pass		

You are West, and the position is:

```
              NORTH
              ♠ A J 10 9 8
              ♥ J 8 7
              ♦ J
              ♣ Q 6 5 3

    WEST
    ♠ K 5 3
    ♥ A Q 6
    ♦ 6 5 4
    ♣ J 7 4 2
```

You lead the club two, and your partner wins with the king and returns the heart two. Plan your defence.

2. You open one diamond and your partner is silent. The opponents reach four spades, and you are West in this position:

> NORTH
> ♠ A 7 4
> ♥ A 9 8 7
> ♦ 5 3
> ♣ J 9 7 2

> WEST
> ♠ K Q 10
> ♥ 4
> ♦ K J 10 6 2
> ♣ A K 10 6

You lead the club king, getting the three from your partner and the queen from declarer. You try the spade king, which is allowed to win. What next?

3. You are West, defending four hearts in the following situation:

> NORTH
> ♠ Q 10 5 4
> ♥ A 10 9
> ♦ 6
> ♣ K J 10 7 2

> WEST
> ♠ A 6 2
> ♥ J
> ♦ J 9 8 5 4 3
> ♣ A 9 4

You lead a diamond, and your partner wins with the ace. South plays the king. East returns a trump, and South takes two trump tricks, one with the ace in dummy and one with the king in his hand. What do you do if South then leads the club five?

4. You know the opponents are using five-card majors and the bidding has been:

South	West	North	East
1 ♦	1 NT	Pass	Pass
Dbl.	Pass	2 ♦	Dbl.
Pass	Pass	Pass	

Your hand and dummy are:

NORTH
♠ J 8 2
♥ 9 4
♦ 10 8 5 3
♣ Q 8 5 4

WEST
♠ K Q 3
♥ A J 2
♦ Q 9 2
♣ K 9 7 2

You have led the diamond two. What distribution do you think the declarer has?

5. South has opened one no-trump (16–18 points), been raised to two and continued to three. West leads the heart two, and as East you can see:

NORTH
♠ 9 5 3
♥ 6 4
♦ A K 10 8 2
♣ 9 8 5

EAST
♠ 8 2
♥ A Q 10 7 5
♦ 5 3
♣ J 10 7 4

Plan your defence.

6. The bidding goes:

East	South	West	North
1 ♦	1 ♠	2 ♣	2 ♥
Pass	2 ♠	3 ♣	Pass
Pass	3 ♥	Pass	3 ♠
Pass	4 ♠	Dbl.	Pass
Pass	Pass		

You are East. Your partner leads the diamond four, and you can see:

NORTH
♠ Q 8
♥ A J 9 8 4
♦ Q 10 3 2
♣ J 5

EAST
♠ A 9 4
♥ 5 2
♦ A J 9 8 7 5
♣ K 3

South ruffs your diamond ace. Plan your defence if declarer now:
(a) leads the spade ten, on which your partner and dummy play low;
(b) leads a low club to dummy's jack, your partner playing low.

7. You unwisely double a contract of six no-trumps, and can see the following after the opening lead:

NORTH
♠ Q 3
♥ K Q
♦ 8 7 3
♣ A J 10 5 4 3

WEST
♠ K 8 7 5 2
♥ J 9
♦ A J 4
♣ 7 6 2

The bidding has shown that South has a balanced hand with 17 or 18 points. Your passive club lead is won by dummy's ten. Plan your defence if the declarer next leads a diamond to his king.

8. Both sides are vulnerable, and the bidding goes:

East	South	West	North
1 ♥	3 ♦	3 ♥	Pass
Pass	4 ♣	Pass	4 ♥
Pass	6 ♣	Pass	Pass
Pass			

The West and North hands are:

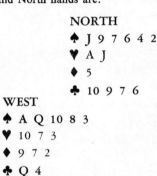

NORTH
♠ J 9 7 6 4 2
♥ A J
♦ 5
♣ 10 9 7 6

WEST
♠ A Q 10 8 3
♥ 10 7 3
♦ 9 7 2
♣ Q 4

As West you lead the spade ace, on which your partner plays the king and South the five. What do you lead now?

9. You are West after the following auction:

West	North	East	South
1 ♦	Pass	Pass	1 ♥
Dbl.	Redbl.	2 ♦	3 ♣
Pass	4 ♥	Pass	Pass
Pass			

NORTH
♠ J 8 4 2
♥ Q J 8 5
♦ 4 3
♣ A Q 5

WEST
♠ A K 10 5
♥ K
♦ K J 9 7 5
♣ K J 6

You lead the spade king, on which East plays the three and South the seven. What next?

10. As East you have made three straight penalty doubles, all of them unsound, and wind up defending six clubs doubled after the following auction:

South	West	North	East
Pass	1 ♠	Dbl.	Pass
2 NT	4 ♦	Dbl.	4 ♠
4 NT	Pass	5 ♥	Dbl.
Pass	Pass	5 NT	Dbl.
6 ♣	Pass	Pass	Dbl.
Pass	Pass	Pass	

Your partner leads the diamond king, and you can see:

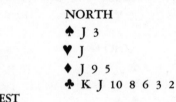

NORTH
♠ 7
♥ A K 10 9 7 3
♦ A 4
♣ K Q 9 8

EAST
♠ 8 3 2
♥ Q J 8 2
♦ 2
♣ 7 5 4 3 2

Plan your defence as East when the declarer wins with the diamond ace and plays a second diamond.

11. You are West, defending four spades in the following situation:

NORTH
♠ J 3
♥ J
♦ J 9 5
♣ K J 10 8 6 3 2

WEST
♠ K 8 2
♥ K
♦ K 10 6 3
♣ Q 9 7 5 4

Your partner has overcalled North's three-club opening with three hearts and you, therefore, lead the heart king. South wins with the ace and leads a small heart. What do you do?

12. As East you double your right-hand opponent's third-seat opening of one club. Your left-hand opponent jumps to two no-trumps and is raised to game. Your partner leads the heart two and you can see:

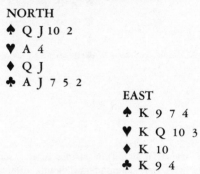

NORTH
♠ Q J 10 2
♥ A 4
♦ Q J
♣ A J 7 5 2

EAST
♠ K 9 7 4
♥ K Q 10 3
♦ K 10
♣ K 9 4

South ducks in dummy and you win the queen and return the three, driving out the ace. South leads the diamond queen from dummy, and when you play the king it wins. You cash two heart winners, collecting South's jack on the third round. What now?

13. Your side does not bid, and your opponents reach a slam:

South	North
1 ♠	2 ♦
2 ♥	3 ♠
4 NT	5 ♦
6 ♠	Pass

After the opening lead of the club two, as East, you can see:

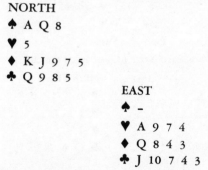

NORTH
♠ A Q 8
♥ 5
♦ K J 9 7 5
♣ Q 9 8 5

EAST
♠ –
♥ A 9 7 4
♦ Q 8 4 3
♣ J 10 7 4 3

South plays low from dummy and takes your ten with the ace. He leads the diamond ten to dummy's king (West following with the six) and leads the heart five. What do you do?

14. You are East in the following situation:

NORTH
- ♠ A 7 4
- ♥ A 9 8 7
- ♦ 5 3
- ♣ J 9 7 2

EAST
- ♠ 8 3
- ♥ J 10 6 2
- ♦ 9 7 4
- ♣ 8 5 4 3

You are defending four spades after your partner has opened the bidding with one diamond and South, after two passes, has protected with one spade. Your partner wins the first two tricks with the club king and the spade king. He switches to the heart four, and your ten is taken by declarer's king. A trump is led to the ace, your partner playing the ten, and the declarer wins two heart tricks with the eight and queen, West playing two low diamonds. On a trump lead your partner plays the queen. What do you now discard holding:

- ♠ –
- ♥ 6
- ♦ 9 7 4
- ♣ 8 5 4

15. The bidding goes:

East	South	West	North
1 ♦	2 ♥ (weak)	2 NT	3 ♥
Pass	4 ♥	Dbl.	Pass
Pass	Pass		

You are East. Your partner leads the club two, and you can see:

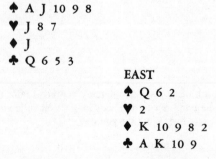

NORTH
- ♠ A J 10 9 8
- ♥ J 8 7
- ♦ J
- ♣ Q 6 5 3

EAST
- ♠ Q 6 2
- ♥ 2
- ♦ K 10 9 8 2
- ♣ A K 10 9

You win with the club king and switch to the trump two. West takes the queen and ace of hearts and plays a third heart, removing dummy's trumps. South wins and plays a spade. Your partner plays the king, and South wins with the ace and returns the jack. Do you play the queen? And on what do you base your decision?

16. You are East, defending six clubs which North bid in response to one club.

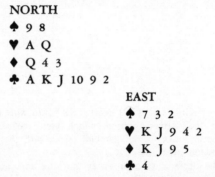

NORTH
♠ 9 8
♥ A Q
♦ Q 4 3
♣ A K J 10 9 2

EAST
♠ 7 3 2
♥ K J 9 4 2
♦ K J 9 5
♣ 4

Your partner leads the spade queen. South wins with the ace and plays three rounds of trumps. Your partner produces one trump and discards the spade five and the diamond two. What do you discard?

17. The bidding goes:

South	West	North	East
1 ♦	Pass	2 ♣	Pass
2 NT	Pass	3 NT	Pass
Pass	Pass		

You are East. West leads the spade five, and you can see:

NORTH
♠ J 9 4
♥ A 6 3
♦ 9 6 2
♣ A Q 10 9

EAST
♠ K 10
♥ K 8 5 4
♦ 7 4
♣ J 8 7 5 2

What do you play if the declarer plays low from the dummy?

18. North bids six no-trumps in reply to his partner's one no-trump opening bid (15–18 points) and you can see.

NORTH
♠ 6 4
♥ A K 7 3
♦ A 10 6
♣ A Q 7 2

EAST
♠ J 10 5
♥ 6 4
♦ 8 7 4 2
♣ 9 8 4 3

The opening lead is the heart jack. South wins with the heart queen and leads the diamond queen, which your partner covers with the king. Declarer makes three diamond tricks with the ace, jack and ten, West following each time.

The declarer then produces the king and jack of clubs, making four tricks in that suit. West follows twice and then discards two spades. On the last club South throws a spade. He then cashes dummy's top hearts, reducing the dummy to two spades and the heart seven. What should your last three cards be?

Answers

1. You need to plan well ahead here. The first stage is surely to remove dummy's trumps, so score yourself 10 points for planning to continue trumps, taking two winners and then leading the six. The second stage concerns the spade suit: when South leads low you must be ready to play the king.

This unusual second-hand-high play will cut South's communications if he has exactly two small spades. If he has any other holding your play will not affect the issue. (The chance that South has four small spades is too slight to worry about.) **Score 10 bonus points for planning to play the spade king.**

(See hand 19)

2. Lead the heart four, 10 points.

A spade or a diamond lead is almost sure to give the declarer a trick. South's club queen is liable to be a singleton, so another club lead is dangerous. The heart lead can hardly do anything that the declarer will not be able to do for himself.

(See hand 24)

3. Play low without hesitation, 10 points.

The declarer probably has a guess in clubs, so you should not guess for him by winning the ace, or even by thinking about winning. Even if the declarer has a singleton and guesses to play the king from dummy you may not lose in the long run.

(See hand 26)

4. The declarer's distribution is surely 4-4-3-2, 10 points.

East must have three trumps to make a penalty double of two diamonds. This leaves the declarer with only three diamonds, and an opening bid in a three-card diamond suit is only indicated when a player has precisely four cards in each major, three diamonds and two clubs when he has an even distribution with the wrong count for one no-trump. (See hand 10)

5. Play the heart ace and continue the suit, 10 points.

The play of the queen, with the idea of driving out South's hypothetical king, is right in some similar situations. But in this case it is cunning rather than clever. It can gain in the rather unlikely situation in which your partner has led from J x x. But it will often lose because your partner will not know he should continue hearts when he gains the lead. (See hand 45)

6. (a) Allow South to win with the spade ten. If he plays another spade, play the club king intending to continue that suit, 10 points.

Your best chance is that your partner has a six-card club suit headed by the ace—quite likely on the bidding—and that you can collect a trick with the spade nine on the third round of clubs. You must, therefore, try to win the second trump lead with the ace, so that dummy's trump queen will not be available for South to play on the third round of clubs.

(b) Take the club king and lead a low spade, 10 points.

Your only hope is to remove one trump from the dummy. This still gives you a chance of making your spade nine on the third round of clubs if the declarer slips. (See hand 43)

7. Win and return a diamond (the jack or the four), 10 points.

There is a faint chance that your partner has the queen. If he has the ten but not the queen the diamond play may break up a squeeze position. If he has neither diamond honour you are probably going to be endplayed anyway, thanks to your foolish double. (See hand 41)

8. The spade queen, 10 points; a lesser spade or a heart, 3.

One chance is that partner has the club jack and will ruff with it to promote your club queen. Another is that South has the club jack and will misguess the queen after a passive heart switch. The spade queen takes care of both chances—East can ruff if he has the club jack, for it costs him nothing, and he will not be tempted to ruff if he does not have that card. (See hand 21)

9. Lead the diamond king, 10 points.
When your partner passed one diamond, he showed a very weak hand, probably less than five points. If you lead a low diamond and your partner plays the queen, the declarer is likely to work out that you have the heart king. By leading the diamond king you can keep your partner's queen concealed, and the declarer is likely to take a normal heart finesse. (See hand 47)

10. Ruff the diamond lead—in spite of the fact that your partner will win the trick if you discard.
It is vital for you to gain the lead and play a trump to reduce the impact of South's impending cross-ruff, **10 points.**

(See hand 39)

11. Discard a club or a diamond, 10 points.
The trap to avoid is ruffing with the spade eight, a card that you will need later in the defence. A sad fate may await you if you fall into that temptation. (See hand 28)

12. Lead the spade king, 10 points.
The indications are that South has a long diamond suit, and he must have the spade ace as a side-entry. The entry must be attacked before South can unblock his diamonds, even if the play sacrifices a trick or two. (See hand 23)

13. Play low, 10 points, and do it quickly.
Second-hand high in this type of position is far more likely to help the declarer than to hurt him. If you hesitate even for a second you will tip him off to the winning play if he has a king-jack combination. (See hand 32)

14. A club, 10 points; a heart, 9.
Although it is generally right to keep four cards in dummy's suit, there is no possible advantage here. With the ace still out your eight cannot possibly beat dummy's nine on the fourth round of the suit. The club is, therefore, useless and the heart virtually useless. However the diamond holding might have a value.

(See hand 24)

15. If your partner has a singleton king of spades South has four and it will not matter whether you take your queen now or later.
So you must assume that your partner has made an expert defensive play by putting up the king from K x or K x x. The latter

is slightly more likely, so you should play your queen at once, **10 points.** If your partner held a doubleton king of spades he might well have led it originally in the hope of obtaining a ruff. You know that he had a trump to spare for ruffing purposes, and the risk involved in the spade lead would be quite slight since you had opened the bidding. (See hand 19)

16. The heart two and any other low card (spade two, heart four or diamond five) in any order, 10 points.
Do not signal to show either of your red kings. The information may help the declarer, but cannot possibly help your partner. He has nothing to do except keep his spade stopper. (See hand 25)

17. Spade king, 10 points.
There is a conflict here between the need to establish partner's spades and the need not to give South a trick. The play of the spade king apparently gives South a trick if he has the ace. But the play of the spade ten is likely to leave the spades blocked. It is vital to play the king if West has the ace but not the queen, and the king can still be right, for unblocking reasons, at the cost of a trick, if West has a five-card suit headed by the queen.
(See hand 44)

18. Two spades and the 'useless' thirteenth diamond, 10 points.
Your only hope is that your partner has the spade king together with a heart stopper. If that is so he will be endplayed by the lead of the last heart—unless you leave South guessing about the location of the last diamond. (See hand 42)

Awards

160–200	OUTSTANDING
120–150	VERY GOOD INDEED
80–110	AVERAGE
40–70	FAIR
0–30	POOR

The Final Assessment

NATIONAL CHAMPION 1500–1800
EXPERT 1200–1499
MASTER 900–1199
INTERMEDIATE 600–899
HOME PLAYER 300–599
NOVICE 0–299

If you have completed all the quizzes and kept a record of your score, congratulations. You are now a better player than when you began.

I estimate that very few players would score well enough to reach the top two categories. Most good players would find themselves with a 'Master' rating or even in the 'Intermediate' division.

Most players lacking serious bridge experience will find themselves rated as 'home player' or 'novice'. Do not be surprised if this is the case. Put the book away for a few weeks and then try the quizzes again. I predict that you will improve your score, and this will demonstrate that your game is on the way up.

SECTION TWO

THE STORIES

Behind the Answers

The Sunday columns in *The New York Times*, from which the hands given in this section of the book are selected, are designed to present an instructional point about the game. In doing so other angles on bidding and play inevitably creep in. All these have been explored in the quizzes in Section One, so readers who have conscientiously worked through the quizzes will have a feeling of déjà vu in many cases. They should find, in consequence, that they can readily understand many complex points about the game.

Judging the Bidding

A Natural Invitation to a Slam

♠ Q J 4
♥ K Q 9 8 3
♦ J
♣ 9 8 4 2

HAND
NO. 1

♠ A 8 3 2
♥ 10 7 6 2
♦ Q 9 6
♣ 7 3

NORTH
WEST — EAST
SOUTH

♠ 7
♥ A J 5 4
♦ 10 8 4 3 2
♣ J 10 5

♠ K 10 9 6 5
♥ –
♦ A K 7 5
♣ A K Q 6

Both sides vulnerable

South (D)	West	North	East
1 ♠	Pass	2 ♠	Pass
5 ♠	Pass	6 ♠	Pass
Pass	Pass		

West led the club seven

Many players delight in devising or adopting new artificial conventions, confusing not only their opponents but also their partners in the process. They would perhaps be better occupied in making sure that they have a full understanding of natural bidding sequences.

There is one entirely natural bid which is seldom used, perhaps because players do not think of it or because they do not understand its meaning: the direct slam invitation made by bidding five of the agreed major suit. This can have two meanings according to circumstances.

When there is exactly one unbid suit, five of the intended trump suits asks for control of the unbid suit. In other situations the direct invitation means 'I have no problems in the side suits, but I am afraid we may have two losers in our trump suit.' The responder is then guided by his trump holding in deciding whether to bid a slam.

South has a spectacular opportunity to use this bid on the diagrammed deal, reported by the German expert, Dr Ulrich Auhagen. His hand does not justify a forcing opening bid, but becomes enormously powerful when North raises to two spades. A slam should be an excellent bet if North has some strength in spades, so the jump to five spades is indicated.

North judges that his queen-jack of spades will help to fill the gap in his partner's trump suit and continues to six spades. West leads the club seven, which is covered by the eight, ten and king.

South would give a lot to have one more trump in the dummy. As it is, he has a good deal of work to do to make the slam. Clearly he must ruff at least one of his losing diamonds in the dummy, and the question is whether he should take both diamond winners immediately.

In the interests of keeping control, it is best to take the diamond ace only, risking the possibility that the king will be ruffed eventually. A low diamond is ruffed at the third trick, and the heart king is played from dummy.

East covers with the ace, and South ruffs. A low spade is led, and dummy's queen wins, leaving this position:

```
                      NORTH
                      ♠ J
                      ♥ Q 9 8 3
     WEST             ♦ -              EAST
     ♠ A 8 3          ♣ 9 4 2          ♠ -
     ♥ 10 6 2                          ♥ J 5 4
     ♦ Q              SOUTH            ♦ 10 8 4
     ♣ 3              ♠ K 10 9         ♣ J 5
                      ♥ -
                      ♦ K 7
                      ♣ A Q 6
```

An impulsive declarer will seize the opportunity to discard his losing diamond on the heart queen. He will play a trump, over-taking the jack with the king, and his contract will fail because the trumps break badly. West will win and lead a heart, so South loses control of the trump suit.

South must think a little harder in the diagrammed position. He should realise that he has no chance if the club suit does not break: there is no way to draw trumps and get back to dummy for a finesse against East's presumed club jack.

If the clubs are breaking, that suit provides a long-term entry back to the dummy, so there is no hurry to cash the heart queen. South must lead the spade jack, overtaking with the king in his own hand. However West plays, the trumps can be drawn, and South eventually returns to dummy with the fourth round of clubs to cash the heart queen.

Notice that an expert player in the East seat might defeat the contract. South's unusual five-spade bid strongly suggests first-round control of all the side-suits, and if East appreciates this point, he will play low quickly when the heart king is led from dummy. South would then attempt a cross-ruff and be defeated by the four-one trump break.

Bid to Be Dummy—If That's Your Rightful Role

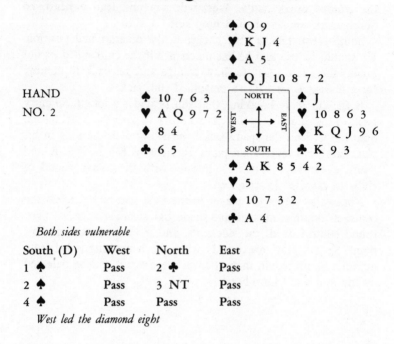

HAND NO. 2

```
                    ♠ Q 9
                    ♥ K J 4
                    ♦ A 5
                    ♣ Q J 10 8 7 2
        ♠ 10 7 6 3                    ♠ J
        ♥ A Q 9 7 2                   ♥ 10 8 6 3
        ♦ 8 4                         ♦ K Q J 9 6
        ♣ 6 5                         ♣ K 9 3
                    ♠ A K 8 5 4 2
                    ♥ 5
                    ♦ 10 7 3 2
                    ♣ A 4
```

Both sides vulnerable

South (D)	West	North	East
1 ♠	Pass	2 ♣	Pass
2 ♠	Pass	3 NT	Pass
4 ♠	Pass	Pass	Pass

West led the diamond eight

An accurate assessment of one's own ability is sometimes a practical, if painful, necessity for a bridge player and it is, therefore, unfortunate that almost all players above the beginner stage have an inflated idea of their own talents. The modest player is a rare bird.

The point is important in rubber bridge if two players of unequal ability find themselves in partnership. The best results will be obtained if the weaker player becomes the dummy much more often than his partner, but this will only work out well if both players are alert and adjust the bidding accordingly.

On the diagrammed deal, played at the Regency Whist Club, North, the weaker player, failed to make the appropriately modest rebid at his second turn. After South had rebid his spade suit a raise to four spades is the right *theoretical* bid with the North hand. For it is highly probable that South has six spades —with only five he might well have been able to find a more descriptive rebid by showing a red suit, raising clubs or bidding two no-trumps. North's doubleton queen is sufficient support for a six-card suit.

Four spades was also the right *practical* bid to steer the declaration into the South hand. North could have taken into account the fact that his partner was Theodore Lightner, one of the world's great players. Lightner, who played regularly with Ely Culbertson in the early days of the game, has contributed substantially to the development of bidding theory. Although he celebrated his 75th birthday in 1968, he still plays a difficult hand as well as anyone, and showed it on this deal.

When North bid three no-trumps on the second round, Lightner had a difficult decision. Three no-trumps might have been the right contract—North could have had a singleton spade —but South followed the rule: when in doubt, make the better player the declarer. He put the team into the proper contract of four spades.

The opening diamond lead was won in dummy, and the club queen was led for a successful finesse. Dummy's remaining diamond was led, preparing the way for a diamond ruff, and when East won with the jack he returned the spade jack. The declarer won in dummy with the spade queen, and came to his hand with the club ace. The position was now this:

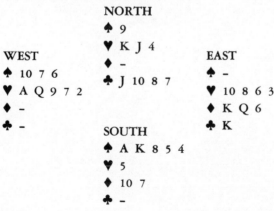

```
                    NORTH
                    ♠ 9
                    ♥ K J 4
     WEST           ♦ -              EAST
     ♠ 10 7 6       ♣ J 10 8 7       ♠ -
     ♥ A Q 9 7 2                     ♥ 10 8 6 3
     ♦ -                             ♦ K Q 6
     ♣ -                             ♣ K
                    SOUTH
                    ♠ A K 8 5 4
                    ♥ 5
                    ♦ 10 7
                    ♣ -
```

At this point the average player would ruff a diamond and start thinking. Thinking would not help him, for there would be no way to make the contract. For example, if he then ruffed a club low, West would overruff, cash the heart ace, and exit with a trump.

Foreseeing this difficulty, Lightner found a remarkable way to make his contract. He led his singleton heart, forcing West to put up the heart ace. West did the best he could by returning the spade ten, sacrificing a trump trick but removing the nine from dummy and apparently leaving South with two diamond losers.

This was good defence, but Lightner had the last laugh. He took the king and ace of spades, but instead of drawing the last trump with the eight, he led the four. West was forced into the lead with the trump seven and had to lead a heart. Dummy's jack was finessed, and both South's diamond losers disappeared.

Needless to say, North was impressed—and even modest enough by then to acknowledge he wouldn't have found the winning play.

A Modern Rule for Pre-emptive Bidding

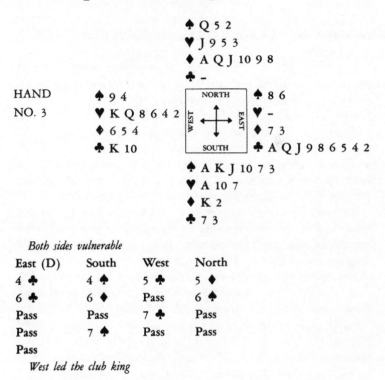

HAND NO. 3

```
                              ♠ Q 5 2
                              ♥ J 9 5 3
                              ♦ A Q J 10 9 8
                              ♣ -
        ♠ 9 4          NORTH         ♠ 8 6
        ♥ K Q 8 6 4 2  WEST   EAST   ♥ -
        ♦ 6 5 4                       ♦ 7 3
        ♣ K 10         SOUTH         ♣ A Q J 9 8 6 5 4 2
                              ♠ A K J 10 7 3
                              ♥ A 10 7
                              ♦ K 2
                              ♣ 7 3
```

Both sides vulnerable

East (D)	South	West	North
4 ♣	4 ♠	5 ♣	5 ♦
6 ♣	6 ♦	Pass	6 ♠
Pass	Pass	7 ♣	Pass
Pass	7 ♠	Pass	Pass
Pass			

West led the club king

The textbooks have an easy rule for pre-emptive bids, known as 'the rule of two and three'. A player who opens with a bid of three or more in a suit is expected to be within two tricks of his contract if vulnerable and within three tricks not vulnerable.

But this simple way is not for the experts. Experienced players will make pre-emptive bids much more freely than the textbook rule would suggest, and will take into account the opposing vulnerability as well as their own. The experts practice what might be called 'the rule of two, three, four and five'. It works this way.

If the dealer is vulnerable and the opponents are not—the most dangerous position to take pre-emptive action—he should have seven probable tricks, or two short of his contract, to make a three-bid.

If both sides are vulnerable he should have six probable tricks, perhaps A Q J x x x x or K Q J x x x x. This is three tricks short of his contract.

If neither side is vulnerable, a more broken seven-card suit or a strong six-card suit would be acceptable: A J x x x x x or K Q J x x x. These represent five likely tricks, and the opening bidder is, therefore, four tricks short of his contract.

Finally, at favourable vulnerability the opening bid can be completely frivolous. Some experts would make a three bid when not vulnerable against vulnerable opponents with a suit as weak as Q x x x x x x or K J 10 x x x. These have about four playing tricks, and are five tricks short of the contract.

The risks involved in aggressive pre-emptive bidding are not great, and the possible rewards, by crowding the proceedings for the opposition, are considerable. The gigantic swing on the diagrammed deal from a Wisconsin tournament was largely due to the decision of two different dealers on how high to pre-empt.

At one table East opened four clubs—rather too timid a bid since it allowed South to overcall four spades and let North bid his diamonds at the level of five (or cue-bid six clubs, a good alternative). East-West tried to save in seven clubs over six spades, which North would have doubled if he had no interest in his own slam. His pass, however, was an invitation to bid seven, and South was happy to accept.

As it happened seven spades could have been defeated by an opening heart lead, which East would ruff, and seven diamonds would have been unbeatable. But this was an accident which North-South could not foresee: with nine spades in the combined hands and only eight diamonds, spades appeared to be safer.

East might have tried a Lightner double of seven spades—a signal to prevent his partner from leading a club—but West would still not have been sure about leading a heart. With many partnerships the double would call for a diamond lead— i.e. dummy's first suit—and as diamonds had been bid and supported West might suppose that his partner was void and looking for a lead there. Instead, the lead was the club king and South claimed 13 tricks, giving him 2,210 points.

This contrasted with the result at another table after East opened five clubs, a more sensible bid than four clubs because he could anticipate eight tricks and was only three short of making five.

The opponents' bidding was jammed: South had to bid spades at the five level, West interposed a six-club bid and North was forced to six spades. East bid seven clubs, and South had a problem. Knowing nothing about the diamonds, he didn't dare pass, which would invite a grand slam from North; he wasn't sure enough to bid the slam on his own; and so he had to double.

Now it was South's turn to find the wrong lead. It seemed quite likely from their aggressive bidding that one of the opponents would be able to ruff spades, so he opened the heart ace. This gift was a pleasure to East, who ruffed and led to the club king. A low heart was ruffed in the closed hand, and a second trump lead to the ten in dummy drew the missing trumps. East's diamond and spade losers were discarded on the established hearts and the grand slam was made for a score of 2,330.

Two grand slams made in opposite directions on the same deal for a total score of 4,540 points may be some sort of record. And both of them could have been defeated.

The DOPI Convention— How to Avoid Bidding a Grand Slam Missing an Ace

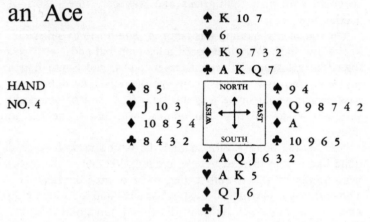

HAND
NO. 4

North and South vulnerable

South (D)	West	North	East
1 ♠	Pass	2 ♦	Pass
3 ♠	Pass	4 NT	5 ♥
5 NT	Pass	6 ♣	Pass
6 ♦	Pass	7 ♠	Pass
Pass	Pass		

West led the diamond four

To bid a grand slam missing an ace that the opponents can cash at the first trick might seem a gross error which easily can be avoided by beginners who have learned to use the Blackwood Convention. Yet, it has happened twice in world championships in an eight-year period, and in similar circumstances.

In 1962 this writer, playing for Great Britain, was the sufferer, reaching a hopeless seven-heart contract missing the diamond ace. The disaster was a direct result of an imaginative bid of five spades by the Texan expert, G. Robert Nail. My partner and I had failed to agree on a procedure to cope with this rare eventuality, and the swing of 16 international match points gave the United States victory in the match.

The traditional solution is to pass with no ace, make a one-step bid with one ace, and so on, reserving a double for penalties. This method has two disadvantages. If the responder doubles, his partner is left in the dark about the number of aces facing him. And if the responder bids, the Blackwood bidder is deprived of the opportunity to penalise his daring opponent.

A theoretical improvement has gained currency in tournament circles recently. The responder doubles with no ace or two aces, passes with one ace or three aces. This double-zero-pass-one system is referred to as DOPI, pronounced dopey. The alternative, neither better nor worse, is to double with an odd number of aces and pass with an even number. Double-odd-pass-even becomes DOPE on the convention card.

Two French players who rank as one of the world's top partnerships may decide to adopt an understanding of this kind after the debacle they suffered on the diagrammed deal in the 1969 world championship. With the North-South cards they held, a contract of six spades would have been good and six no-trumps even better, because the possibility of a diamond ruff is prevented. But their smooth progress towards the small slam was interrupted when Giorgio Belladonna of Rome, sitting East, put in a dashing five-heart bid when North bid Blackwood.

The five no-trumps bid was obviously meant to show two aces, because it was 'two steps' from the five-heart overcall, but North did not understand it that way. The subsequent bids of six clubs and six diamonds were apparently bred of confusion and doubt: 'I am not sure whether we should bid a grand slam, partner, and I hope you know.'

As it happened, the foolish grand slam contract was not easy to defeat, because East held the diamond ace and West was on lead. Walter Avarelli, long Belladonna's partner on the famous Italian Blue Team, thought for some time and finally came up with the winning answer by leading a diamond.

He had good technical reasons for this choice. A trump lead was pointless, and he was sure that North-South would not bid seven missing the ace of East's suit. If East had wanted a club lead he could have doubled North's bid of six clubs. That left only diamonds.

The lead swung 30 international match points, and gave Italy victory in the match by 15 victory points to 5. With any other lead South would have been able to discard his losing diamonds on dummy's clubs, and France would have won the match by 13 points to 7.

The French were a little unhappy about the situation because Belladonna had hesitated slightly before passing seven spades. A double at this point would have asked for a lead of dummy's original suit, so if Avarelli had noticed the hesitation he might have considered himself barred from leading diamonds.

The French players were much more unhappy about their bidding misunderstanding. They now realise that all regular partnerships should agree on how to solve this problem. So if you run into this trouble, don't be surprised if your partner tells you: 'You're a dope not to use DOPI,' or 'You're dopey no to use DOPE.'

The Case of the Nonbarking Bidder

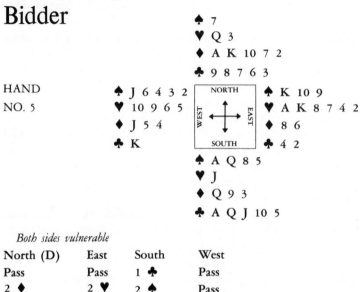

	♠ 7	
	♥ Q 3	
	♦ A K 10 7 2	
	♣ 9 8 7 6 3	

HAND
NO. 5

WEST	NORTH	EAST
♠ J 6 4 3 2		♠ K 10 9
♥ 10 9 6 5		♥ A K 8 7 4 2
♦ J 5 4		♦ 8 6
♣ K	SOUTH	♣ 4 2

	♠ A Q 8 5	
	♥ J	
	♦ Q 9 3	
	♣ A Q J 10 5	

Both sides vulnerable

North (D)	East	South	West
Pass	Pass	1 ♣	Pass
2 ♦	2 ♥	2 ♠	Pass
4 ♣	Pass	4 NT	Pass
5 ♦	Pass	6 ♣	Pass
Pass	Pass		

West led the heart five

Students of Sherlock Holmes will recall the occasion on which the great detective—who might have been a great contract player—made use of a negative inference. In the case of the stolen race horse, Silver Blaize, he advised Dr Watson to note the curious behaviour of the watchdog in the night. The dog's failure to bark suggested that the thief had not been a stranger.

Bridge players often fail to bark in the bidding, giving shrewd opponents considerable opportunity for negative inferences. On the diagrammed deal from the Tri-State Regional Championships at Grossinger's, New York, in 1969, the declarer had an unusual chance to develop a negative inference, and a defender had an even more unusual opportunity to draw a red herring across declarer's trail.

South was able to open one club after two passes because East did not choose to open the bidding with a borderline hand. North's jump response of two diamonds is worth noting: as he has already denied an opening bid, the jump switch should indicate a hand with a good fit with the opener's suit. Many tournament players treat the bid as forcing, with the proviso that the bidding may die if the opener shows a minimum or subminimum hand by rebidding his original suit.

East introduced his heart suit belatedly at the two-level, and South showed his secondary spade suit. North continued his kangaroo-like progress by jumping to four clubs, a bid that would have been justified if his useless heart queen had been in one of the minor suits.

South could reasonably expect that the club slam would be no worse than a finesse, so he used Blackwood to make quite sure that there were not two aces missing.

A heart was led to the king, and South ruffed the heart ace with the club ten at the second trick. He led the spade ace and ruffed a spade, noting that East followed with the nine and ten.

The obvious play was to lead the club nine for a finesse, which is clearly the right play of the club suit on a percentage basis. But South felt he could afford to postpone the decision in trumps. The fact that there had been little barking—sorry, bidding—suggested in a general way that the side suits would break fairly evenly. It was certainly unlikely that West had started with ♠ K J x x x x, for he would no doubt have entered the auction with a weak jump overcall, a heart raise, or a double of two spades.

South, therefore, took the very slight risk of entering his hand by leading to the diamond queen and ruffing a third round of spades. The appearance of the king from East then gave him a vital clue. East had shown up already with a long heart suit headed by the ace-king, and now produced the spade king. As he had passed originally, there was an overwhelming inference that he did not have the club king. On this basis, South's only hope was that West held the singleton club king, so he led to the club ace and made his slam. There is no point in taking a finesse that you know will lose.

East missed the chance to be brilliant. He could have concealed the heart king, and prevented South from drawing his negative inference, by winning the first trick with the heart ace and returning a low heart. South's bidding, not to mention West's lead of the heart five, virtually guaranteed that South did not have two hearts, so the risk in such a play was negligible.

With the misleading indication that the heart king was in the West hand, South would certainly have failed in the slam. He would have ruffed the second heart lead, entered dummy, and taken the normal club finesse. And lost the contract.

Happiness Is a Double Fit

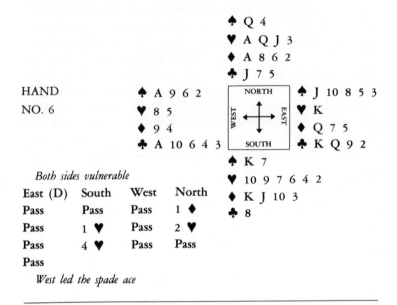

	♠ Q 4
	♥ A Q J 3
	♦ A 8 6 2
	♣ J 7 5

HAND ♠ A 9 6 2   NORTH   ♠ J 10 8 5 3
NO. 6   ♥ 8 5   WEST — EAST   ♥ K
 ♦ 9 4   SOUTH   ♦ Q 7 5
 ♣ A 10 6 4 3   ♣ K Q 9 2
 ♠ K 7
 ♥ 10 9 7 6 4 2
 ♦ K J 10 3
 ♣ 8

Both sides vulnerable

East (D)	South	West	North
Pass	Pass	Pass	1 ♦
Pass	1 ♥	Pass	2 ♥
Pass	4 ♥	Pass	Pass
Pass			

West led the spade ace

Most players realise that they are entitled to get excited when the bidding indicates that the partnership has a good fit in one suit. But they do not always appreciate that they are entitled to be doubly excited when there is a double fit—that is, a fit in two suits.

This consideration was the key to South's bidding on the diagrammed deal, played in the Spingold Knockout Team Championship in Los Angeles in 1969. His 7-point hand suddenly took on a golden hue after two rounds of bidding.

North's opening bid after three passes was one diamond rather than one heart, because a major-suit bid would have promised a five-card suit in his methods. South reviewed the situation when his one-heart response was raised to two hearts.

With a double fit known to exist in the red suits, South judged correctly that his game prospects were excellent. He assumed that he would lose one trick in each of the black suits, and not more than one trick in the red suits.

On this basis he jumped to four hearts, a bid with a two-way purpose. The double fit indicated not only that North-South had good prospects of making game, but also that East-West would do well in the black suits. As it turned out, East-West would have made nine tricks in a spade contract. South was, therefore, not worried about the danger of defeat in four hearts—if that contract failed, it was likely that East-West would have missed at least a part-score in spades.

After West had led the spade ace, South inspected the dummy and discovered that his bidding assessment was accurate: he had a sure loser in each of the black suits, and a possible loser in each of the red suits.

East played the spade three on the first trick to discourage a spade continuation, and West switched to the club ace. This time East played the encouraging nine, so West played a second club and South ruffed.

The obvious play for South was to finesse in trumps, hoping to make a winning guess in the diamond suit if the finesse failed. But a little thought showed South that this would not be the right play.

West had already produced two aces, and it was not likely that he held the heart king: with two aces and a king he would probably have opened the bidding or taken action on the second round.

Moreover, if West did have the heart king, South could make his contract without finessing. In view of the original passes, West could not have two aces, a king and a queen, so if West showed up with the heart king, the diamond queen would be marked in the East hand.

Fortified by this analysis, South led to the heart ace in dummy and was gratified when the king fell from East. The declarer was now in the happy position of being sure of 10 tricks. The guess in diamonds represented an overtrick possibility, and South made the winning guess by finessing against East.

If the heart king had not fallen, South planned to ruff dummy's remaining club, cash the spade king, and lead a trump. If West had won, the diamond finesse would have been taken against East.

South could have been left with a headache if East had won

the second trump lead. The hypothetical position would then have been:

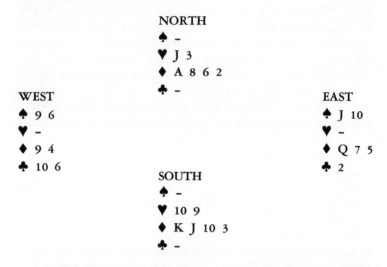

NORTH
♠ –
♥ J 3
♦ A 8 6 2
♣ –

WEST
♠ 9 6
♥ –
♦ 9 4
♣ 10 6

EAST
♠ J 10
♥ –
♦ Q 7 5
♣ 2

SOUTH
♠ –
♥ 10 9
♦ K J 10 3
♣ –

The best defence in this position would be for East to lead a black card, conceding a ruff-and-discard. South would still have had to guess the situation of the diamond queen.

As it was, the contract was made and East and West realised too late that they should have entered the bidding and reached four spades. They screamed at each other until both were on the verge of apoplexy; whereupon South was able to diagnose another variety of double fit.

The 'Splinter' Bid Solves the Problem of Duplication

HAND
NO. 7

```
            ♠ J 10 5 3
            ♥ 10
            ♦ A Q J 9
            ♣ Q J 8 5

♠ Q 9 7 4    NORTH    ♠ K 8 2
♥ 8 7 3 2  WEST EAST  ♥ A K J 9
♦ 7 5 4              ♦ 2
♣ 10 7      SOUTH     ♣ K 9 6 4 2

            ♠ A 6
            ♥ Q 6 5 4
            ♦ K 10 8 6 3
            ♣ A 3
```

Neither side vulnerable

West (D)	North	East	South
Pass	Pass	1 ♣	1 ♦
Pass	3 ♥	Dbl.	5 ♦
Pass	Pass	Pass	

West led the club ten

In the original version of this book, marks were awarded in the Quiz sections for the use of 'Splinter Bids'. These were deleted when preparing the Anglicised version, as being hardly known to British players yet. They remain, however, of considerable interest in this 'Stories Behind the Answers' section.

Tournament players love duplicate but hate duplication. Duplication, that is, of winning tricks, is when one player has an ace and his partner a void, thus giving them two sure ways to win but a single trick. Unproductive overkill, that.

One way to detect duplication is now popular with many American tournament experts. A player who wishes to show that he is very short in a particular suit can do so in some situations by making an unusual jump bid, known as a 'Splinter Bid'.

This will usually mean skipping two levels:

Opener	Responder
1 ♣	1 ♠
4 ♦	

The four-diamond bid announces a hand with a fine spade fit, enough strength to play in game and at most one diamond. The responder can then evaluate the slam chances knowing that he can discount honour cards in diamonds other than the ace. If he has no interest in slam, he simply signs off with four spades.

This shortage-showing jump bid has been called a 'splinter' bid, to distinguish it from the 'fragment' jump used by a few American experts to show a holding of two or three cards in such situations. The splinter has a wide variety of applications, and was the key to North-South's success on the diagrammed deal. It was played in the quarter-final round of the Spingold National Team Championship in Minneapolis in 1969. The deal accounted for more than the eventual margin of victory for B. Jay Becker's New York team, which went on to reach the final.

Once North had passed and East had opened one club, Dorothy Hayden (now my wife), sitting South, had little thought of reaching game when she overcalled one diamond. But the picture changed completely when Becker, as North, made an unusual jump to three hearts—a splinter bid promising a powerful diamond fit, game prospects and not more than one heart.

South could discount her heart queen, which was clearly a worthless card opposite a singleton or void heart. But she had good control of the other three suits and made a bold jump to five diamonds. Everyone passed, and the opening lead was the club ten.

The declarer covered the ten with dummy's club jack, which won the trick, and led the heart ten. East put up the heart king and returned a club, which South took with her ace. She had lost the heart and knew she would lose a spade, so to make her contract she had to be able to ruff all her heart losers—not as easy as it might appear.

After South ruffed a heart in dummy, led a spade back to the ace and ruffed another heart, she was left in the dummy with this position:

NORTH
♠ J 10 5
♥ -
♦ A Q
♣ Q 8

WEST
♠ Q 9 7
♥ 8
♦ 7 5 4
♣ -

EAST
♠ K 8
♥ A
♦ 2
♣ K 9 6

SOUTH
♠ 6
♥ Q
♦ K 10 8 6 3
♣ -

The obvious play was to ruff a club and ruff the last heart, but the obvious play would have been fatal. The club ruff would have to be made with the diamond eight to avoid an overruff, and once South ruffed her last heart in dummy, there would be no safe way to return to her own hand to draw trumps. A spade lead would permit East to win and play yet another club, forcing South to ruff high, thus promoting the diamond seven as a trick in the West hand.

Mrs Hayden foresaw the problem and found the right solution. She decided to let the opponents take the spade trick first, opening up a chance for her to ruff a spade as a way to return to her hand. In the diagrammed position she led a spade from the dummy. (Leading a club and discarding a spade would have been equally effective.) East won and led a low club, which was ruffed with the diamond eight. The heart queen was ruffed in dummy, the diamond ace cashed and now South was able to re-enter her hand safely with a spade ruff. She easily drew West's trumps without permitting East to play another club. The splinter bid and careful play had scored the game and won the match.

Resist That Temptation to Double

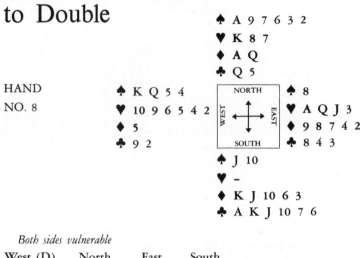

HAND
NO. 8

```
              ♠ A 9 7 6 3 2
              ♥ K 8 7
              ♦ A Q
              ♣ Q 5
♠ K Q 5 4              NORTH          ♠ 8
♥ 10 9 6 5 4 2    WEST ←  → EAST      ♥ A Q J 3
♦ 5                                   ♦ 9 8 7 4 2
♣ 9 2                  SOUTH          ♣ 8 4 3
              ♠ J 10
              ♥ -
              ♦ K J 10 6 3
              ♣ A K J 10 7 6
```

Both sides vulnerable

West (D)	North	East	South
Pass	1 ♠	Pass	2 ♣
Pass	2 NT	Pass	3 ♦
Pass	3 ♠	Pass	4 ♦
Pass	5 ♦	Dbl.	Redbl.
Pass	Pass	Pass	

West led the heart ten

Doubling the opponents in a game or slam contract that they apparently expect to make is an expensive luxury. Greedy players who have this habit fail to realise that the odds are heavily against them. The venturesome doubler may gain an extra 50 or 100 points by beating the declarer by one trick. But if his judgment is wrong, his loss may be anything from 150 to 710. Remember that the opponents may redouble, and the mathematics will be in their favour for such an action.

An even stronger argument against doubling in such situations is that the double will often help the declarer in the play. It may even make the difference between the contract failing and succeeding, in which case the doubler has given away a bushel of points.

This can happen even at world-championship level, as in the dramatic deal shown in the diagram. It was played in 1969 in a match between Brazil and China in Rio de Janeiro, and both teams went astray in the bidding.

When the Brazilians held the North-South cards, they slipped slightly by bidding to six diamonds. This is, of course, an excellent contract, but six clubs is even better. South was certainly unlucky to go down in his contract: he ruffed the opening heart lead and attempted to draw the trumps. With any normal break he would have been able to claim the slam, but the five-one division was a killer. He lost control, and wound up down three.

When the hand was replayed on Bridge-O-Rama, the North-South cards were held by K. W. Shen and Kovit Suchartkul, two Thai experts who were co-opted members of the Chinese team.

They use the 'Bangkok Club' System in which bids of one spade, one heart and one diamond promise a five-card suit. South gave a good picture of his hand by bidding clubs, followed by two bids in diamonds. As this showed 11 cards in the minor suits, North should have realised that his minor-suit honours were enormously valuable. He could have jumped to six clubs, which would have been an easy contract.

Instead North bid five diamonds, reaching the wrong suit just as the Brazilians had done. South was wondering whether to continue to a slam when East chose to double, a greedy action based on his five trumps. This might have driven North-South back into six clubs, but instead South redoubled. Redoubled contracts are very rare in championship play, and this one was exciting for the audience, who could see all the cards on the Bridge-O-Rama screen.

Without any information about the distribution, South would probably have gone down in five diamonds by ruffing the first trick and trying to draw trumps. But it was clear to him that East's only reason for doubling must be length in diamonds, and he was able to take precautions against the bad division.

At the second trick South led to the diamond ace, but instead of continuing trumps he began on clubs, a very fine decision. It would have been a blow to him if West had been able to ruff, but as it was, it was East who ruffed. He shifted to a spade, which was taken by dummy's ace. The diamond queen was overtaken with the king, and South was in control. He drew the remaining trumps, cashed his clubs and lost one trick at the finish.

It would not have helped East to play the heart ace instead of a spade at the seventh trick. South would simply have ruffed and continued with clubs. This way he would lose a second trump trick, but the spade loser can eventually be discarded on the established heart king in dummy.

South scored 950 points for making his contract, and East was left with the realisation that his rash double had cost 1,050 points.

4+4 Is More Than 5+3

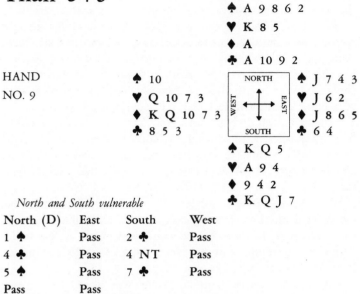

HAND NO. 9

```
                    ♠ A 9 8 6 2
                    ♥ K 8 5
                    ♦ A
                    ♣ A 10 9 2
  ♠ 10                  NORTH        ♠ J 7 4 3
  ♥ Q 10 7 3       WEST ←→ EAST     ♥ J 6 2
  ♦ K Q 10 7 3                       ♦ J 8 6 5
  ♣ 8 5 3              SOUTH         ♣ 6 4
                    ♠ K Q 5
                    ♥ A 9 4
                    ♦ 9 4 2
                    ♣ K Q J 7
```

North and South vulnerable

North (D)	East	South	West
1 ♠	Pass	2 ♣	Pass
4 ♣	Pass	4 NT	Pass
5 ♠	Pass	7 ♣	Pass
Pass	Pass		

West led the diamond king

When suits are equal, one may turn out to be more equal than another. When a partnership has a choice between two possible trump suits in each of which the partnership has eight cards, a four-card fit is often more productive than a five-three fit.

Many textbooks have examples of deals on which the four-four fit is worth one more trick to the declarer. In a New York knockout match the four-four fit was worth two tricks, and it made the difference between a game and a grand slam.

At one table North-South bid to four spades, and North felt foolish when he saw the dummy. A spade slam would seem to be a lay-down, with just one heart trick to be lost, but North was in for a pleasant surprise. The trumps broke four-one, and East made a trump trick, as he was bound to do barring double-dummy play of the spades by North.

North thought that his team might gain on the deal, for there seemed a good chance that the North-South pair on the opposing team would bid six spades and go down. But he had overlooked the possibility that North-South would play in clubs.

After North had opened one spade and heard his partner respond two clubs, he made a well-judged jump to four clubs. Although he was slightly short of high cards for this strong re-bid, his hand was very powerful in terms of distribution and controls. If the hands fitted well there was a distinct possibility of making a slam with less than the usual quota of points.

William Passell of Hartsdale, New York, who held the South hand, was also in a position to judge that the hands would fit well. He visualised North's five spades and four clubs, and knew that all his high cards would pull their weight in a slam.

When South's Blackwood bid produced the information that North held all three missing aces, South went all the way to seven clubs. He foresaw that he would make extra ruffing tricks with clubs as trumps, and that North's spades would give him at least one discard from his own hand.

West led the king of diamonds, which was taken by the ace in dummy. The declarer had to plan carefully. On the face of it he could make 13 tricks by drawing the trumps. With normal breaks in both black suits he could make five spade tricks, three top winners in the red suits, and five trump tricks.

But Passell rightly did not choose to rely on favourable breaks. He devised a line of play which would work if either black suit divided four-one. His first move was to cash the club ace and lead to the club king in his hand. A diamond was ruffed in the dummy and the closed hand was re-entered with a heart lead to the ace.

South's last diamond was ruffed in the dummy, and a spade lead to the king gave South the entry to draw the remaining trump. He still had one trump in his hand, and the heart king remained in dummy as a vital entry. He cashed the spade queen and led to the spade ace. When West showed out, the declarer was happy that he had taken the precaution of ruffing two diamonds in the dummy.

The spade suit was continued and when South ruffed the fourth round he had the heart king and the last spade in the dummy to win the last two tricks and make the grand slam.

Passell's team gained 1,490 points in all, or 16 international match points, winning a comfortable victory. The North-South pair who played in four spades learned a useful lesson about playing in a four-four fit.

Planning the Play

Defenders Can Learn Things if They Listen

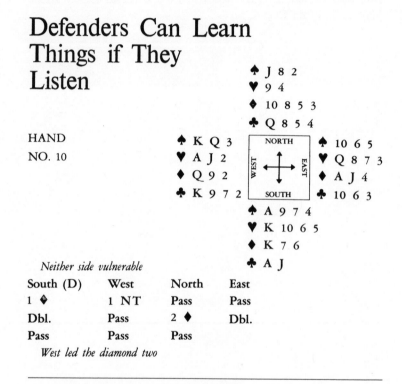

HAND NO. 10

```
                 ♠ J 8 2
                 ♥ 9 4
                 ♦ 10 8 5 3
                 ♣ Q 8 5 4
♠ K Q 3      NORTH      ♠ 10 6 5
♥ A J 2   WEST  EAST    ♥ Q 8 7 3
♦ Q 9 2               ♦ A J 4
♣ K 9 7 2    SOUTH     ♣ 10 6 3
                 ♠ A 9 7 4
                 ♥ K 10 6 5
                 ♦ K 7 6
                 ♣ A J
```

Neither side vulnerable

South (D)	West	North	East
1 ♦	1 NT	Pass	Pass
Dbl.	Pass	2 ♦	Dbl.
Pass	Pass	Pass	

West led the diamond two

Defenders who listen to the bidding can learn a lot. Every bid made by the declaring side carries inferences, both positive and negative. An alert defender can often add clues from the declarer's bidding to the information available to him by looking at his own hand and the dummy and build a mental picture of his opponent's hand. On the diagrammed deal, played in a game in Poughkeepsie, N.Y., West knew the precise distribution of the declarer's hand as soon as the dummy appeared.

South had a wide choice of opening bids. Many in America

would bid one no-trump, even though the hand is a point below the traditional 16-point minimum. A few would bid one spade or one heart, although these suits are rather too flimsy for major-suit opening bids in that country. Another minority would bid one club, carrying the 'short club' concept much too far. Most experts, though, would go along with South's actual one-diamond bid, on a least-evil basis.

West's overcall of one no-trump showed a hand equivalent to a no-trump opening (though really a point short). South's double was clearly out of line, since that indicates 17 points or more, and North could do no better than retreat into two diamonds. East, however, made an alert penalty double, confident that he and his partner held balanced hands with more than their share of top cards.

In normal circumstances one would not consider a trump lead from a holding of Q x x, but in this case West had already started to read the cards. North's weak bidding and East's double gave him good reason to think that East held a trump honour and that it was important to cut down South's ruffing possibilities.

When the dummy came down, West tried further card-reading. He reasoned first that South had only three trumps. After all, East would hardly make a penalty double with less than three diamonds, meaning South could not have four. Second, he knew that a player who opens a short minor will bid one club rather than one diamond when he has three cards in each suit. So South could have only one distribution to justify his diamond bid: four spades, four hearts, three diamonds and two clubs. With this in mind West was continually able to stay a jump ahead of South.

East won the first trick with the diamond ace and returned the four. South won with the king and led a third diamond, putting West on play with the queen. West saw that he was liable to give South a trick by opening up spades or hearts. But he knew South had a doubleton club (presumably including the ace), so there was nothing to be lost by switching to that suit.

The club switch was won by South with the jack, and he led a low spade with the idea of establishing his 13th spade. West won with his spade queen and led a second club, driving out South's ace. South continued with his spade plan by leading the seven, which West took with his king. A nervous West might have cashed his winning ace of hearts and king of clubs at this point, setting the contract by a single trick, but this West, helped by his knowledge of South's distribution, knew there was no hurry. He quietly exited with his last spade.

South finally got his two spade tricks by overtaking dummy's jack with the ace; West and dummy discarded hearts on his good 13th spade. But then South had to lead a heart from his hand. West won with the jack and led the heart ace, which dummy had to ruff. South was thus forced to lead from dummy's queen-eight of clubs into West's king-nine, and the defenders made the last two tricks.

The result was down two, and the penalty of 300 points gave East-West a top score. If South had been as clever in card-reading as West was he would have found the way to escape for down one. After winning the fourth trick with the club jack he should have cashed the club ace before leading a small spade. This would have deprived West of his exit card and endplayed him immediately.

Every Rule Can Be Bent— or Broken

	♠ J 5 2	
	♥ 10 7 5	
	♦ K 8 7	
	♣ A 10 7 6	

HAND NO. 11

♠ A K 10 9 4	NORTH	♠ 8 3
♥ 8 3 2	WEST ← → EAST	♥ K 9 6 4
♦ 3		♦ Q J 10 9
♣ 9 8 4 2	SOUTH	♣ Q J 5

	♠ Q 7 6	
	♥ A Q J	
	♦ A 6 5 4 2	
	♣ K 3	

East and West vulnerable

West (D)	North	East	South
Pass	Pass	Pass	1 NT*
Pass	2 NT	Pass	3 NT
Pass	Pass	Pass	

West led the spade nine

* Playing 'Strong' throughout.

The general rule for the declarer in a no-trump contract is to develop tricks in the partnership's longest combined suit first. But like every bridge rule this can be bent—or, as in the diagrammed deal from a New York exhibition match, broken. In this case only if the declarer had resisted his longest suit and turned instead to his weakest could he have found the paradoxical winning plan.

South opened the bidding with one no-trump. Though North had only an eight-point hand and thus a borderline raise to two no-trumps, he was influenced by his two tens: intermediate cards often sway the decision between pushing towards game or resting in a part-score. South held only 16 points, the standard minimum for a no-trump opening, but he knew his five-card suit was an asset and continued to game.

West's lead of the spade nine was proper. South played low from dummy and won in his hand with the queen.

Then, without thinking the hand through, he sealed his doom by continuing with the routine play of a low diamond, which he willingly gave up to East. His hope here was that the diamonds would break three-two and the spades four-three, meaning that he would lose only that one diamond and the three outstanding spades. Alas, the hope was not enough. East simply continued the spades and West ran four more tricks to defeat the contract.

South would have done better here if he had thought harder. His 'routine' play could have succeeded only with considerable luck. Not only would the diamonds and spades have to break perfectly, but the heart king would have to be well placed.

The declarer must, therefore, assume that the heart finesse will win, and base his reasoning on that. He has one spade trick at the start, he has four top tricks in the minor suits, and a winning heart finesse will give him a total of eight. The ninth trick will probably come from diamonds, but—and this is the point—there is no hurry for this. In fact, South does best by not committing himself at all in the minor suits until the defenders have taken their tricks. This way he can open up the possibility of a squeeze play at the end, and the general rule of a squeeze play is: tricks that must be lost should be surrendered as quickly as possible.

Therefore, South should not lead diamonds. He can guess that the defenders will presumably make their spade tricks however he plays, and he should not be reluctant to lose those tricks. Thus the winning plan—a very unusual one—is for South to lead his opponents' spade suit at the second trick.

West will then presumably grab his four spade tricks. Before the last one is played the position will be as shown opposite.

On West's last spade the declarer throws a club from dummy. East cannot spare a club and has to let go a diamond. It does not matter what West then leads, but assume he plays a club. South wins in his hand with the king, leads to the diamond king and takes a heart finesse. The heart ace is cashed, dropping the king, and on the third round of hearts a diamond is thrown from dummy.

East is squeezed. He cannot keep his diamond guard and his

club guard, and South must make his ninth trick in one of the minor suits. A triumph for the breaker of general rules.

If West foresees that his partner may be squeezed, he may resist the natural inclination to cash his last spade in the position above. But this does not help the defence. South can give up a club trick to establish the ten in dummy, or he can take three heart tricks, forcing East to part with a diamond, and then give up a diamond trick to establish his ninth trick in that suit.

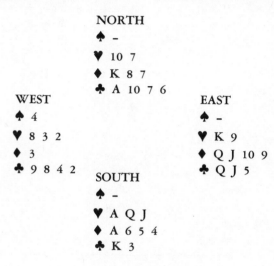

NORTH
♠ –
♥ 10 7
♦ K 8 7
♣ A 10 7 6

WEST
♠ 4
♥ 8 3 2
♦ 3
♣ 9 8 4 2

EAST
♠ –
♥ K 9
♦ Q J 10 9
♣ Q J 5

SOUTH
♠ –
♥ A Q J
♦ A 6 5 4
♣ K 3

The Dangerous Safety Play

HAND
NO. 12

♠ J 8 6 2
♥ 5
♦ J 9 5 4 3
♣ A K 10

♠ A K Q 9 7 4 3
♥ 10 9 8
♦ 10 6
♣ 2

NORTH

WEST — EAST

SOUTH

♠ 5
♥ K 4
♦ K 8 2
♣ Q 9 8 7 5 4 3

♠ 10
♥ A Q J 7 6 3 2
♦ A Q 7
♣ J 6

East and West vulnerable

South (D)	West	North	East
1 ♥	2 ♠*	Pass	Pass
3 ♥	Pass	3 NT	Pass
4 ♥	Pass	Pass	Pass

West led the spade ace
* Weak jump overcall.

The supreme example of tragicomedy in the game of bridge is the 'unsafety play'. A cautious declarer playing a contract which seems very likely to succeed concludes that he can increase his prospects by abandoning any thought of overtricks. He therefore adopts a 'supersafe' line of play, only to find that he has gone down and that a routine approach would have succeeded.

A remarkable case of the 'unsafety play' occurred in a New York tournament. In a knockout team match, East-West suffered a substantial penalty at one table. The opening bid by South on the hand diagrammed above was one heart, and West—in this case—overcalled three spades. North's hand was then ideal for a penalty double: he held a probable trump trick, a singleton in his partner's suit and two quick tricks outside. Those who use the 'negative double' would have been at a disadvantage here.

West had an unhappy time in three spades doubled. The opening lead was the club king, and North switched to his singleton heart. South won and led his spade ten, after which the declarer could do no better than take six trump tricks, down 800 points.

In the post-mortem, East-West noted, as a small silver lining from their angle, that North-South might have been able to make a slam. Suppose that South plays in six hearts, and that two high spades are led. By playing all out and guessing well, South can then make 12 tricks, aided considerably by fortune. He must ruff the second spade and enter dummy with a club lead. A trump finesse allows the trumps to be drawn, with the king falling conveniently under the ace. A problem remains in diamonds, but South should decide that West is more likely to have the ten singleton or doubleton in that suit than East the king as part of a short holding. On that basis South must use his remaining club entry to dummy to lead the diamond jack to make his 12 tricks.

North-South were not alarmed by this analysis. They saw that good defence would defeat the slam, in the unlikely event of the North-South pair for the opposing team reaching such a dizzy height.

After leading a high spade against six hearts, West should appreciate the possibility that his partner might hold a trump honour. The indicated play at the second trick would, therefore, be a low spade, forcing East to ruff. East would ruff as high as possible, hoping to uppercut the declarer, and West's heart ten would become the setting trick if East produced the jack, queen or king.

When the match was over, the teams compared scores. The North player who had doubled three spades was pleased to find that his team-mates were plus 50 on the deal. 'Well done,' he declared, 'I suppose they reached six hearts, and you beat them with the uppercut.'

'Not at all,' responded West. 'They reached four hearts, and we beat that.' As four hearts seemed quite simple to make, North-South were eager to hear the story. In the auction shown with the diagram above, West had heeded the unfavourable vulnerability and bid just two spades, a pre-emptive jump overcall, rather than three spades. South had rebid his hearts and reached game in his suit when his partner tried three no-trumps.

West led the spade ace—and saw little chance of defeating the heart game. He switched to his singleton club, which was won by the king in dummy. South saw that he was likely to lose one diamond and one trump in addition to the spade trick, and there was some danger of losing two trumps.

The safest procedure seemed to be to draw the trumps as quickly as possible. He, therefore, led to the heart ace, rejecting the finesse, and followed with the heart queen. This was a safety play against a singleton king in the West hand and, on the face of it, reduced the danger of a ruff by clearing four trumps speedily from the defending hands.

Unfortunately for South, East won the second trump lead with the king and gave his partner a club ruff—the club two was an obvious singleton. West simply exited with a high spade, and South was forced to lead diamonds from his hand, thereby losing the setting trick.

'I could have made 12 tricks,' announced South sadly, as he conceded a one-trick defeat, 'but I thought I had better play it safe for 10.'

Slow but Sure Wins the Game

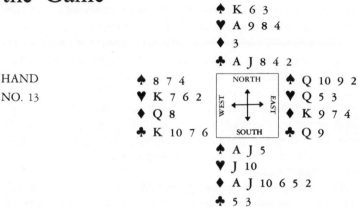

```
              ♠ K 6 3
              ♥ A 9 8 4
              ♦ 3
              ♣ A J 8 4 2
HAND    ♠ 8 7 4      NORTH      ♠ Q 10 9 2
NO. 13  ♥ K 7 6 2   WEST  EAST  ♥ Q 5 3
        ♦ Q 8                   ♦ K 9 7 4
        ♣ K 10 7 6  SOUTH       ♣ Q 9
              ♠ A J 5
              ♥ J 10
              ♦ A J 10 6 5 2
              ♣ 5 3
```

East and West vulnerable

South (D)	West	North	East
1 ♦	Pass	2 ♣	Pass
2 ♦	Pass	2 ♥	Pass
2 NT	Pass	3 NT	Pass
Pass	Pass		

West led the eight of spades

Speedy play does not win any prizes at the bridge table, although there can be penalties in tournaments for those who perform like snails. Nevertheless, there are many players of moderate ability who attack the play of the dummy with such energy that one would suppose they were required to finish in less than a minute.

Experts will often take a full minute before playing from dummy to the first trick. They know the importance of making a careful plan, which South failed to do on the diagrammed deal, played in Sweden.

South had a borderline opening bid of one diamond. Many

players would pass, and some who use weak two-bids would try two diamonds. North bid his hand naturally in response by showing his long club suit followed by the heart suit. South was forced to keep bidding, and rightly showed that he could stop the unbid spade suit by bidding two no-trumps.

North should perhaps have given up at two no-trumps. He had shown a strong hand by bidding two clubs and two hearts, and South would no doubt have jumped to three no-trumps if he had had any reserve strength.

However, North persevered to game and South had to struggle in a precarious contract against the lead of the spade eight. He ran the lead round to his hand, winning with the jack when East played low, and decided that he needed a small miracle in one of the minor suits.

His first move was to lead a low club, inserting dummy's jack when West played low. East won with the queen and continued with the spade queen. South won in dummy with the king and led dummy's singleton diamond. His remaining hope was that East held K Q x in the suit, but West captured the jack with the queen and that was that.

A third spade removed South's ace, and his plans were in ruins. After cashing the diamond ace, he had to struggle to make seven tricks: he ducked a club to East, who eventually had to open up the heart suit. Dummy made two aces and a heart trick, and the contract was down two.

South's line of play would have succeeded if West had held ♣ K Q x or East a similar holding in diamonds. This offered about one chance in seven of making the contract, and he should have looked for something better.

South's best prospects lay in the diamond suit, and he should have concentrated on that. If he had thought before playing from dummy at the first trick, he would have seen that the problem lay in the entries to his own hand. The obvious play of a low card from dummy was wrong in this case: in his eagerness to be quite sure of making three spade tricks, South made it impossible to use his diamond suit.

West's top-of-nothing lead of the spade eight made it likely that East held the spade queen. South should, therefore, have put up dummy's king in order to retain two spade entries to his own hand. His problem then would have been to develop the four diamond tricks, and the obvious play was to lead to the jack. But the winning alternative is to lead to the diamond ace and play a small diamond.

The obvious play fails here, and is slightly wrong theoretically. In the crucial cases when West has a doubleton (in other situations South's choice of play does not affect the result materially), the chances are four to three in favour of the immediate play of the diamond ace.

The second diamond lead is a low card—the jack would be a bad mistake—and West takes the queen. The best he can do is to switch to a low club, and South takes dummy's ace immediately and finesses the spade jack. When this succeeds he is virtually home. He leads the jack of diamonds to establish his suit, and when East wins with the king the defenders are helpless.

Certainly it takes time to work this out, but you must decide what is best for your ego: to have your partner congratulate you on making your contract after considerable cerebration; or to have the opponents admire the speed and confidence with which you misplay the hand.

Miracles Work Both Ways

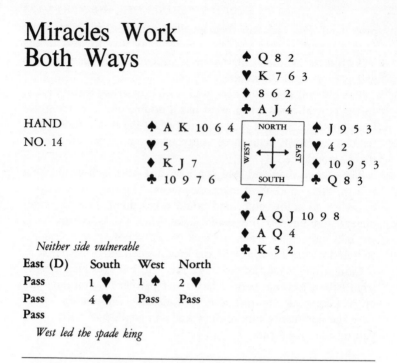

	♠ Q 8 2	
	♥ K 7 6 3	
	♦ 8 6 2	
	♣ A J 4	

HAND NO. 14

♠ A K 10 6 4	NORTH	♠ J 9 5 3
♥ 5	WEST — EAST	♥ 4 2
♦ K J 7	SOUTH	♦ 10 9 5 3
♣ 10 9 7 6		♣ Q 8 3

	♠ 7	
	♥ A Q J 10 9 8	
	♦ A Q 4	
	♣ K 5 2	

Neither side vulnerable

East (D)	South	West	North
Pass	1 ♥	1 ♠	2 ♥
Pass	4 ♥	Pass	Pass
Pass			

West led the spade king

Bridge players are used to miracles. A declarer may profit from a very lucky distribution of the opposing cards. Or he may encounter a 'reverse miracle' with all the luck on the other side. The diagrammed deal illustrates both situations.

Four hearts is a normal contract, and is reached by the sequence shown after West has overcalled one spade. North's raise to two hearts is a slight underbid, and most British players would make the normal limit bid of three hearts. South then has enough to go to game.

West leads the king of spades against four hearts and switches at the second trick to the club ten. South will then go down in his contract unless he prepares for a 'reverse miracle'. He has nine top tricks, and a successful finesse in either clubs or diamonds will produce a tenth. But if luck is with East-West, both finesses will fail.

First consider what happens if the declarer plays in routine fashion. He covers the club ten with the jack in dummy, scowls when East produces the queen, and wins with his king. He draws trumps and finesses in diamonds and ends up losing one spade, two diamonds and a club.

But West's overcall suggests that he has some strength outside spades, so the diamond finesse is likely to fail. If declarer thinks hard enough before playing the second trick, he can work out an endplay possibility and deprive East-West of the benefit of their 'reverse miracle'.

The winning move against any distribution of the opposing cards is to allow West to win the second trick with the club ten. South's aim is to prevent East from winning a club trick, for a diamond lead through the ace-queen would interfere with the plan. West cannot do better at the third trick than persevere with clubs, and South wins with the king.

The black suits must be stripped to prepare the endplay against West. South cashes the heart ace, leads to the heart king in dummy and ruffs a low spade. Finally he leads to the club ace and reaches this position, which sets up West for the kill:

```
                      NORTH
                      ♠ Q
                      ♥ 7 6
      WEST            ♦ 8 6 2        EAST
      ♠ A 10          ♣ -            ♠ J 9
      ♥ -                            ♥ -
      ♦ K J 7         SOUTH          ♦ 10 9 5 3
      ♣ 9             ♠ -            ♣ -
                      ♥ Q J 10
                      ♦ A Q 4
                      ♣ -
```

South leads the spade queen from dummy and discards his diamond loser. West wins with the spade ace and has to make a losing lead. A diamond lead from the king permits South to score the ace and queen. A black-suit lead gives a ruff-and-discard, so South can ruff in dummy and discard the diamond queen.

Now suppose that North-South, by wild overbidding, reach a contract of six hearts. Once again the lead is the spade king and

West switches to the club ten. Clearly the slam is a hopeless proposition with the East-West cards as shown in the diagram.

To make 12 tricks South must hope for a genuine miracle. He assumes, as a starter, that the finesses in clubs and diamonds will both succeed. But there seems no way to avoid the loss of a diamond trick in addition to the spade trick unless West holds five diamonds besides his spade length.

Suppose the East-West cards are:

WEST	EAST
♠ A K 10 6 4	♠ J 9 5 3
♥ –	♥ 5 4 2
♦ J 9 7 5 3	♦ K 10
♣ Q 10 9	♣ 8 7 6 3

With this highly favourable distribution, the declarer can operate a squeeze. He wins the second trick in dummy with the club jack and plays all his six trumps, discarding a spade and a diamond from dummy. Next he cashes the king and ace of clubs and, as West must keep the spade ace, he has to leave himself with only two diamonds. The diamond queen is finessed, and the diamond four makes the last trick in the closed hand.

Sometimes You *Can* Read Through the Back of the Cards

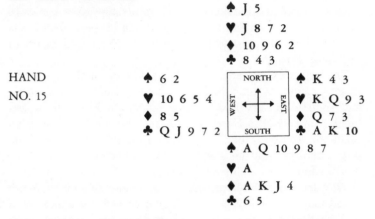

♠ J 5
♥ J 8 7 2
♦ 10 9 6 2
♣ 8 4 3

HAND
NO. 15

♠ 6 2
♥ 10 6 5 4
♦ 8 5
♣ Q J 9 7 2

♠ K 4 3
♥ K Q 9 3
♦ Q 7 3
♣ A K 10

♠ A Q 10 9 8 7
♥ A
♦ A K J 4
♣ 6 5

Neither side vulnerable

East (D)	South	West	North
1 NT	4 ♠	Pass	Pass
Pass			

West led the club queen

A myth prevalent among novice players suggests that the expert 'knows every card you have before you start to play'. This is a gross exaggeration, if one rules out of consideration the opponents of those novices who generously hold their cards well forward in a visible position.

Still, there is something to the novice's belief. It is true that on some deals an expert may remain in doubt about the distribution or the location of the high cards almost until the end of the play. But in most cases he will gradually collect fragments of information, and will know all or nearly all he needs to know after seven or eight tricks have been played. And there are rare hands that suggest that the expert really has X-ray eyes. One such deal, shown in the diagram, was reported by the French periodical 'Le Bridgeur.'

East opened the bidding with one no-trump, showing 16–18 high-card points. As South had 18 points in his own right, it was easy for him to calculate that North and West held hands of negligible strength.

The orthodox procedure for South was to double, expecting to get a chance to jump the bidding subsequently to three spades and so issue a very strong game invitation. However, it was highly unlikely that North would feel able to accept such an invitation, so South took the gamble of jumping immediately to game, knowing that he might fail by two or three tricks if the North hand proved quite unsuitable.

West led the club queen, and on surveying the dummy, South found that he could place every high card with assurance. West had clearly led from a queen-jack combination, revealing three points, and the declarer could count 20 points in his own hand and the dummy. Equally clearly, East held all the missing 17 points. If West held a second queen, East could not have the 16 points he had shown by his opening bid.

This calculation helped South to form the winning plan when the defenders continued clubs and he ruffed the third round. He was in the happy position of knowing that the finesses in spades and diamonds would both succeed, but, less happily, had no clear-cut entry to the dummy to take any finesse.

The obvious chance—not a very good one—was that the diamond queen would fall doubleton. The declarer naturally looked for something better, and found it.

Dummy had two key cards, the spade jack and the diamond ten. Both were potential entries for the purpose of finessing in the other suit. At the second trick South led the spade queen, hoping that East would win and so promote the spade jack as an entry to the dummy for a diamond finesse.

East played well by refusing to win, and the spade jack was now useless for entry purposes. So South fell back on his second entry-making plan by leading the diamond jack. East could not afford to refuse this trick, for he would then leave his queen insufficiently guarded.

East, therefore, won with the diamond queen and led the heart king. South won with the ace, led to the diamond ten and took the spade finesse to capture the king and make his contract.

The key to the play was to attempt to give East a trick as quickly as possible. South could have done equally well by leading the diamond jack at the fourth trick. East would have been forced to win, and the diamond ten would have served as an entry to dummy to take the spade finesse.

South had to assume that both spades and diamonds would break three-two. If the diamonds had split four-one, he would have had no chance, because the attempt to reach dummy with the second round of the suit would have run into a ruff by West. And if East had held four trumps, he would have made both the spade king and the diamond queen, provided he did not permit the spade jack to become an entry to dummy. The diamond entry would not help the declarer, because the spade king would be immune to capture by finesse.

Notice that the contract would have failed if South had played the spade ace or a high diamond at the fourth trick. His reconstruction of the hand from the bidding stood him in good stead.

Don't Just Sit There— Make Some Assumptions!

```
              ♠ 9 7 2
              ♥ Q 9 6
              ♦ 10 7
              ♣ Q J 10 7 2
```

HAND NO. 16

```
♠ Q 6              ┌─ NORTH ─┐      ♠ J 10 5
♥ A 10 8 4 3 2   W │    ↑    │ E    ♥ J 7 5
♦ K Q 8 3 2      E │ ←───→   │ A    ♦ J 6 5 4
♣ -              S │    ↓    │ S    ♣ K 8 4
                 T └─ SOUTH ─┘ T
                  ♠ A K 8 4 3
                  ♥ K
                  ♦ A 9
                  ♣ A 9 6 5 3
```

Both sides vulnerable

South (D)	West	North	East
1 ♠	2 ♥	Pass	Pass
3 ♣	3 ♦	3 ♠	Pass
4 ♠	Pass	Pass	Pass

West led the diamond king

Note: When you met this hand earlier, top marks were given to an opening bid of one club.

Bridge players do not need to be mathematicians—second-grade arithmetic is quite sufficient for the purposes of practical play—but both bridge players and mathematicians require a capacity for logical thought. The mathematician can often reach a useful conclusion by making an assumption. 'If this is true, then it follows that ...' is a line of thinking that also can help the declarer at the bridge table.

The diagrammed example of this mental approach was played many years ago in a National Championship by Helen Sobel Smith, whose death in 1969 at the age of 59 deprived the bridge world of its greatest woman star.

Mrs Sobel, as she was known for most of her bridge career, opened the South hand with one spade. It is arguable whether such hands should be opened with one spade or one club; many experts would bid one club with the idea of bidding spades twice at a low level to complete a distributional picture.

One advantage of bidding one spade is that it may make it more difficult for the opponents to bid the red suits, but in this case West was strong enough to bid hearts at the two-level, and subsequently diamonds at the three-level.

North's belated raise to three spades is worth noting. He knew from the bidding that South held at least five spades, and that spades would be a satisfactory trump suit. Many players would be tempted by the excellent club support to raise that suit, but in such cases the major suit bid is almost invariably better than the minor.

South had a close decision whether to go on to game, for she knew that the North hand would be weak: North's failure to bid two spades on the first round was significant. But if you are one of the world's best card-players, and your opponents are of lesser calibre, some optimism is acceptable in the bidding. So Helen Sobel continued to four spades when a lesser mortal might have been right to pass.

The prospects seemed poor when West led the diamond king and the dummy appeared. There were three inevitable losers: a diamond, a heart and a trump. A four-one trump break was sure to be disastrous, so South made the necessary assumption that the trumps would divide normally. She had some ground for optimism, too, for East no doubt would have doubled four spades with Q J 10 x in trumps.

Most declarers would reach the first stage in the thought process—the assumption that the trumps must break for any chance of success at all—but would not make the next step in the chain of reasoning: if the trumps break, then West must be void in clubs. West has bid vulnerable at the two-level and the three-level without any sign of life from his partner. His suits are not solid, for South can see the diamond ace and the king-queen of hearts. Therefore, the reasoning goes, and so reasoned Mrs Sobel, West must have 11 cards in the red suits. A five-five distribution would not justify his bidding. So with 11 cards in the red suits and two trumps, West has to be void in clubs. Therefore, the reasoning continues, the club finesse will succeed if South can gain entry to the dummy, but there is also the danger of a club ruff.

It was important to South that East should not gain the lead to give West a club ruff, so she allowed the diamond king to win the first trick. West cashed the heart ace, collecting South's king, and switched back to diamonds.

South won with the ace of diamonds and cashed the spade ace, on which West made the routine—and disastrous—play of the six. South seized the opportunity to lead a small trump, and West found himself forced to make a fatal lead. Whether he led a heart or a diamond South could reach the dummy and finesse in clubs to make her contract.

If West's spade holding had been queen-jack doubleton, the throw-in play would have succeeded against any defence. As it was, an alert West could have saved the day by dropping the queen under the ace of spades. Such a play could hardly lose, for even if East held ♠ J x x the declarer would not be able to reach the dummy for a finesse.

However, West's defence would not have hurt him against a less able declarer. Mrs Sobel demonstrated the importance of making logical assumptions in assessing distribution and planning the play of the hand.

In a Squeeze, a Bad Break Can Be a Good Deal

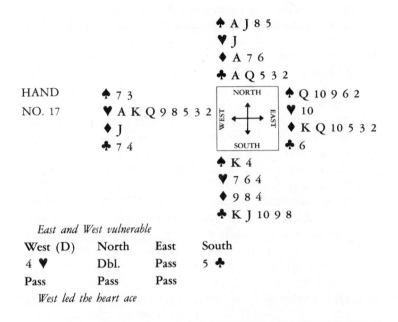

	♠ A J 8 5	
	♥ J	
	♦ A 7 6	
	♣ A Q 5 3 2	

HAND NO. 17

West: ♠ 7 3 ♥ A K Q 9 8 5 3 2 ♦ J ♣ 7 4

East: ♠ Q 10 9 6 2 ♥ 10 ♦ K Q 10 5 3 2 ♣ 6

South: ♠ K 4 ♥ 7 6 4 ♦ 9 8 4 ♣ K J 10 9 8

East and West vulnerable

West (D)	North	East	South
4 ♥	Dbl.	Pass	5 ♣
Pass	Pass	Pass	

West led the heart ace

Not in real life, of course, but most assuredly in bridge, a bad break can be a blessing in disguise. The declarer who prays for even distribution of the opposing cards on weekdays may find himself praying for uneven distribution on Sundays. Consider this everyday situation:

> Dummy
> ♣ A K 6 5
> Declarer
> ♣ 4 3 2

Normally the declarer will hope for a three-three division of the suit, in which case a simple ducking play will produce three tricks. But if he must have four tricks, and there is the possibility of a squeeze, a three-three break may be fatal to his chances. If the suit is unevenly divided, only one defender can guard it. And if that defender is trying to guard another suit, too, he may be susceptible to pressure from declarer.

In the diagrammed deal, the declarer praying for a bad break was Victor Mitchell of New York. He was playing for a team of United States international stars in an exhibition match against Omar Sharif's Circus, a group of European experts headed by the famous movie actor and including two Italian world champions.

In Great Britain most tournament players would prefer to use four no-trumps for a take-out over a major and an optional double over four of a minor. Mitchell, however, sitting South, faced a difficult bidding problem when West's opening bid of four hearts was doubled by North and passed by East. This double was optional in character, and Mitchell could have passed. He knew, however, that Claude Delmouly of France, sitting on his left, is a cautious bidder, and would have at least eight sure tricks in his hand for a four-bid at unfavourable vulnerability. Mitchell chose to take out to five clubs.

Hearts were led and continued, and South ruffed high in dummy. It seemed to the audience of several hundred enthusiasts watching on Bridge-O-Rama that the contract must fail, since South appears to have two inevitable diamond losers in addition to the heart trick. But Mitchell showed them some of the wizardry that permits a great player to make tricks without straw.

He drew trumps in two rounds and led a diamond himself, ducking in dummy. East overtook his partner's jack with the queen and played the king to drive out the ace. South led a trump to his hand, ruffed his last heart with dummy's last trump. He entered his hand with the spade king and cashed his last two trumps, discarding a diamond and a spade.

At the finish, dummy held the ace-jack of spades and South the diamond nine and the spade four. Sharif, sitting East, could not retain his guards in both spades and diamonds. The contract was made.

The bad break in diamonds was the key to South's success. If

West had held three diamonds, he could have retained a guard in that suit, and East would not have been squeezed. The opening bid had given South, quite curiously, grounds for pessimism in spades but for optimism in diamonds. Once West was known to have great length in hearts, the spade finesse was likely to lose, but for the same reason West was unlikely to have three diamonds. And if East had to guard both spades and diamonds, the squeeze was a certainty.

When the deal was over, West pointed out that he could have broken up the squeeze by switching to the diamond jack at the second trick. South could not duck without giving East the opportunity to overtake and give his partner a diamond ruff, and if the ace was played immediately there would be no way for declarer to surrender one diamond trick without surrendering two.

This was good analysis, but Mitchell had an answer. 'If I play you for a singleton diamond,' he pointed out, 'I can still make it. I win the diamond ace, draw trumps and ruff a heart. I cash the king and ace of spades and ruff a spade. This leaves West with nothing but hearts, so when I lead a heart and throw a diamond from dummy, he must give me a ruff-and-discard.'

The gods of bridge had a small shock in store for Mitchell before the match was done. They answered his prayers for a bad diamond distribution, allowing him to make his contract; but when the hand was replayed, his team-mates went down two, doubled, in a four-heart contract—and Sharif's squad gained 3 international match points on the exchange.

A Novice Cashes Winners —An Expert May Do the Same

```
                          ♠ A K 9 3
                          ♥ 2
                          ♦ A Q 8 6
                          ♣ J 10 5 3
```

HAND
NO. 18

```
          ♠ Q 6 5        NORTH        ♠ 8 4 2
          ♥ A Q J 8   WEST     EAST   ♥ 10 6 5 4
          ♦ 9 7 3                     ♦ J 10
          ♣ A 9 4        SOUTH        ♣ K 8 7 2
                          ♠ J 10 7
                          ♥ K 9 7 3
                          ♦ K 5 4 2
                          ♣ Q 6
```

Both sides vulnerable

East (D)	South	West	North
Pass	Pass	1 ♥	Dbl.
2 ♥	2 NT	Pass	3 NT
Pass	Pass	Pass	

West led the diamond nine

An impatience to cash obvious winners in the early stages of a no-trump contract is generally the mark of a beginner. Consider this position:

Dummy

♣ A Q 4 3

Declarer

♣ K J 5

A player who immediately cashes his four club tricks in this situation deprives himself of entries which he may need in the later play, thereby making life easier for the defenders.

Nevertheless, there are deals on which the best policy is to cash winners and hope to scramble for a trick or two at the finish, and the diagrammed deal is a case in point. It was played in the American Contract Bridge League's nationwide charity game in 1969.

Even experts who bar opening bids with four-card major suits would make an exception with the West hand: in third seat, with

a minimum hand, it is important to make the bid which will
direct the best opening lead.

South has a crucial bid to make over two hearts, when his
partner has doubled and East has raised. He could make a
simple bid of three diamonds, which leads to a safe contract. He
could try a penalty double, which leads to a one-trick defeat:
West can lead the heart ten from dummy, which is covered by
the king, and the finesse of the eight later limits the losers to
three spades, two diamonds and one club.

But an aggressive player in the South position will try two no-
trumps, inviting game, and will have a fight on his hands for
nine tricks when his optimistic partner continues to game.

South's two no-trumps bid suggests that he has the heart king,
so West avoids a heart lead. The inspired choice would be a low
club, after which the defenders can take five immediate tricks if
East takes the club king and returns the heart ten—three hearts
and two clubs.

But in practice, West is likely to select a diamond lead as the
least damaging to the defence. It is easy to see that South can
take four diamond tricks and four spade tricks (trapping the
queen), but the ninth trick is not so easy to find. If declarer
makes the normal play of attempting to develop a club trick, he
gives East a chance to make the killing play of the heart ten.

South should diagnose that this is one of the rare situations in
which cashing winners may embarrass the defenders. He takes
the first trick with the diamond king and proceeds to win four
spades and three diamonds, leaving this position:

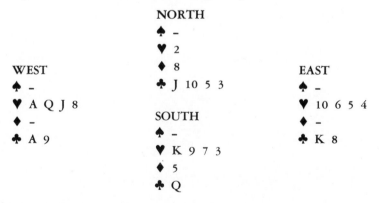

```
                      NORTH
                      ♠ -
                      ♥ 2
                      ♦ 8
    WEST              ♣ J 10 5 3          EAST
    ♠ -                                   ♠ -
    ♥ A Q J 8                             ♥ 10 6 5 4
    ♦ -               SOUTH               ♦ -
    ♣ A 9             ♠ -                 ♣ K 8
                      ♥ K 9 7 3
                      ♦ 5
                      ♣ Q
```

The moment of truth comes with the lead of the diamond eight from dummy. East throws a heart, South plays his diamond and West is squeezed in a strange way.

There are three possibilities for West. He can discard the club nine, but this is obviously fatal: a club lead throws him in and permits the declarer to score the heart king as the ninth trick.

West's second possibility is to throw the heart eight, but this does not help him avoid an endplay in the long run. South leads a club, and sooner or later East has the opportunity to make one heart lead. West eventually has to cash the heart ace and give declarer the heart king.

Finally, West can discard the queen or jack of hearts, but the result is the same. A club is led, and the defenders take the ace followed by the king. East can lead the heart ten, but South covers and finally makes his ninth trick with the heart nine.

Thus it turns out that the only way for South to make his contract is to cash his winners immediately, thereby flying in the face of what is normally the wisest course. The secret, naturally, is knowing when to buck the tide.

How to Defend

Do Not Ignore the Flashing-Yellow Bid

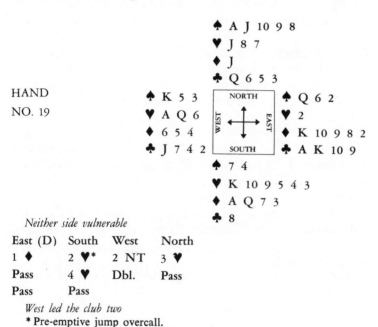

HAND
NO. 19

North:
♠ A J 10 9 8
♥ J 8 7
♦ J
♣ Q 6 5 3

West:
♠ K 5 3
♥ A Q 6
♦ 6 5 4
♣ J 7 4 2

East:
♠ Q 6 2
♥ 2
♦ K 10 9 8 2
♣ A K 10 9

South:
♠ 7 4
♥ K 10 9 5 4 3
♦ A Q 7 3
♣ 8

Neither side vulnerable

East (D)	South	West	North
1 ♦	2 ♥*	2 NT	3 ♥
Pass	4 ♥	Dbl.	Pass
Pass	Pass		

West led the club two
* Pre-emptive jump overcall.

Some bridge bids resemble traffic lights. You can instruct your partner to stop by making a red bid, or signal him to keep moving with a green bid. Sometimes the message may be to slow down and proceed with great caution, and North's bid here might be called a flashing-yellow bid:

South	West	North
1 ♣	1 NT	2 ♥

The two-heart bid suggests length and strength in hearts—five or, more likely, six cards—but no more than about 8 high-card points. If North held a hand with high-card strength and any serious prospects he would double one no-trump.

In any competitive auction when a player rejects a chance to double a no-trump bid, he is flashing yellow. He implies that his side does not have the majority of the high-card strength, and that further bidding is inadvisable. It is a very helpful kind of warning.

South ignored this warning to his cost in the diagrammed deal, which was played in New York in exhibition matches won by Omar Sharif's Circus, a team of visiting European stars headed by the movie actor. East and West were Giorgio Bella-donna and Benito Garozzo, the two Italian world champions, and they exacted a full price for South's misdemeanour.

South's jump to two hearts over one diamond was a weak jump overcall, suggesting a six-card suit and less than the strength needed for an opening bid. West, with a double stopper in hearts and honours in the black suits, invited a no-trump game by bidding two no-trumps, but the invitation had no appeal for East in view of his minimum hand.

North's three-heart bid was entirely reasonable in view of his three trumps—a six-three heart fit was virtually assured—and his ace and singleton. He could envision eight tricks and thought the gamble worthwhile.

But South was certainly wrong in bidding four hearts. He expected to be favoured by a diamond lead, giving him two diamond tricks followed by two diamond ruffs, but this was over-optimistic. He also neglected the discouraging nature of North's flashing-yellow raise and the possibility that West's two no-trumps bid meant he had two heart tricks.

West disappointed South by leading the club two. He had recognised that South's unusual action in continuing to game with a weak hand must be based on the expectation that a diamond lead would help him. The club lead opened the way for a brilliant defence which held South to seven tricks.

East put up the club king, winning the first trick, and shifted to his singleton trump to cut down dummy's ruffing power. West took two trump tricks and led a third round, using up North's trumps and preventing South from ruffing even one diamond in the dummy.

Even so, South still hoped to make eight tricks—or even more—by developing spades. But he reckoned without Garozzo in the West position. When South led a spade at the fifth trick Garozzo put up the spade king, a fine defensive manoeuvre designed to clear the dummy of entries as quickly as possible. Garozzo had to assume that his partner held the spade queen, in which case his own king was expendable on the first trick. A normal second-hand-low play, which would allow South to finesse the ten, would have left East with the awful choice of giving South four spade tricks by winning or two spade tricks by ducking.

Ducking the king would not have helped, so South won with the ace in dummy and continued with the spade jack to try to set up the suit. East decided—rightly—to go up with the spade queen, reasoning that South had held two spades and was unable to get back to the dummy. He reasoned that if West had held the doubleton instead of South he would have led it originally in the hope of a third-round ruff.

East then led the diamond king, killing dummy's jack and South's hopes of reaching the table. South had no escape from losing two diamond tricks at the finish, and was down three for a loss of 500 points. South learned the hard way to respect his partner's flashing-yellow bids.

When the Going Gets Rough, Don't Always Overruff

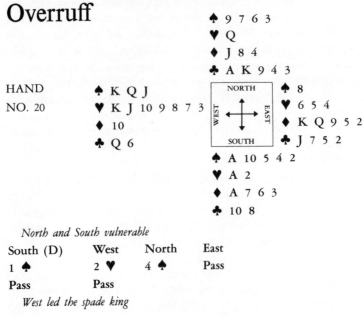

HAND
NO. 20

	NORTH	
♠ 9 7 6 3		
♥ Q		
♦ J 8 4		
♣ A K 9 4 3		

♠ K Q J	♠ 8
♥ K J 10 9 8 7 3	♥ 6 5 4
♦ 10	♦ K Q 9 5 2
♣ Q 6	♣ J 7 5 2

♠ A 10 5 4 2
♥ A 2
♦ A 7 6 3
♣ 10 8

North and South vulnerable

South (D)	West	North	East
1 ♠	2 ♥	4 ♠	Pass
Pass	Pass		

West led the spade king

The average defender seizes with glee on any opportunity to overruff—it's like playing an ace, only more exciting because often unexpected and usually cheaper—but there are some positions in which this is a mistake.

In the diagrammed deal from the 1968 World Team Olympiad in Deauville, France, the advantage to be gained by refusing to overruff was hard to spot. But the Canadian expert sitting West would have defeated the contract if he had avoided the 'obvious' play and refused to overruff.

The bidding was brief. After South had opened with one spade, West overcalled with two hearts, and North, taking a chance, jumped to game in spades.

West led the spade king, and South chose to duck. The spade jack was continued, and South won with the ace. He knew he was doomed to lose a second trump trick, and there would seem to be no escape from two diamond losers—down one. But declarer Tony Trad, a key member of the formidable Swiss team, with brilliant play and a little help from West managed to make 10 tricks.

South's best chance was to find a three-three club break and establish two club winners in the dummy, so he led clubs at the third trick, took the ace and king, and ruffed the third round. West made the obvious play of overruffing and the obvious return of the heart king. His eagerness to take the overruff and his automatic return doomed the defence.

South took the heart king with the ace, ruffed a heart, and ruffed another club. He had lost two, taken six, and the position was:

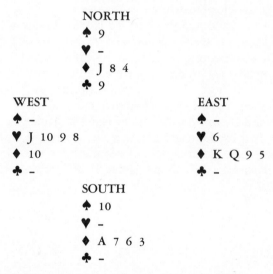

```
                NORTH
                ♠ 9
                ♥ -
                ♦ J 8 4
                ♣ 9
WEST                            EAST
♠ -                             ♠ -
♥ J 10 9 8                      ♥ 6
♦ 10                            ♦ K Q 9 5
♣ -                             ♣ -
                SOUTH
                ♠ 10
                ♥ -
                ♦ A 7 6 3
                ♣ -
```

At this point South had to pray that West had begun with a doubleton king-queen of diamonds or a singleton honour, hoping desperately for an endplay. He led the diamond three and played low from dummy when West produced the ten.

Now the defence was helpless: South could not be prevented from making the last four tricks and his contract. If West held the trick with the diamond ten, he would have to lead a heart next, giving South a ruff and discard, declarer could then throw off one of the dummy's diamonds, trump in his hand, play the ace of diamonds and ruff a small one, ending in the dummy to cash the 13th club. And if East tried to save his partner by overtaking the ten with the queen or king, he too would be endplayed, having to concede a ruff and discard if he led hearts or letting dummy's jack of diamonds win a trick if he led diamonds.

If West had seen what was coming—and, in fairness, it was not all that easy to foresee—he could have saved himself by refusing to overruff the third round of clubs. This would allow him control over the trumps and the declarer could not then afford to concede a trick to the diamond ten in the end position, because West would have been able to cash his spade winner, drawing trumps, and make the remaining tricks, all good hearts. A switch to the diamond ten after the overruff would also have saved the day for the defence.

When the hand was replayed the bidding began in the same way, with a one-spade opening and an overcall of two hearts. The Canadian jumped to three spades rather than four, a jump which invites game rather than forces it in the style of most experts on both sides of the Atlantic. East then tried four hearts, and as South had a minimum opening bid in terms of high cards and good defensive possibilities he chose to double. A good decision—four spades could not be made against the best defence and four hearts doubled was set two tricks for a penalty of 300. Switzerland gained eight international match points on the deal.

Watch for this Defence—
It's a Knockout

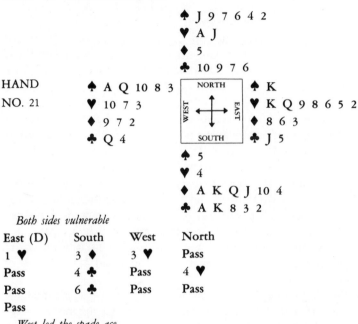

♠ J 9 7 6 4 2
♥ A J
♦ 5
♣ 10 9 7 6

HAND

NO. 21

♠ A Q 10 8 3
♥ 10 7 3
♦ 9 7 2
♣ Q 4

NORTH

WEST EAST

SOUTH

♠ K
♥ K Q 9 8 6 5 2
♦ 8 6 3
♣ J 5

♠ 5
♥ 4
♦ A K Q J 10 4
♣ A K 8 3 2

Both sides vulnerable

East (D)	South	West	North
1 ♥	3 ♦	3 ♥	Pass
Pass	4 ♣	Pass	4 ♥
Pass	6 ♣	Pass	Pass
Pass			

West led the spade ace

The 'uppercut' is surely the most descriptive term in the vocabulary of bridge. A declarer who thinks he is making his contract without trouble may find himself on the receiving end of a knockout blow in this type of position:

NORTH

♠ K 8 4

WEST

♠ J 9 5

EAST

♠ 10 6

SOUTH

♠ A Q 7 3 2

This is the trump suit, and South is ready to draw trumps and claim his contract. But West has the lead, so he leads a suit in which East and South are now void. East plays the spade 10 on the general theory that it cannot hurt and may help his partner. There is no way South can avoid the loss of a trump trick. South overruffs, but, left with only two honours, has to lose a trick to West. South has been uppercut.

An opportunity for an uppercut occurred in the diagrammed deal from a European Championship match played in 1967 between Germany and Switzerland. Most players would open three hearts with the East hand, but the German player chose to bid one heart with less than the normal high-card requirements. South's jump overcall of three diamonds hardly did justice to his enormous playing potential, even playing that bid as strong, in the European style. In American methods a cue bid of two hearts over one heart would be justified.

North did not choose to bid three spades over West's three hearts, but he came to life on the next round when his partner bid four clubs. The cue bid of four hearts showed first-round control of the opponents' suit and implied that his hand had become more promising because of a club fit: the failure to support diamonds on the first round indicated North's lack of interest in that suit.

South jumped to six clubs knowing that he would find the heart ace and club support opposite him, but dummy's trumps turned out to be less substantial than he had expected. When the spade ace was led the contract appeared to depend on finding an even trump division.

West had to do some careful pondering at the second trick. He could see no real hope of making a heart trick, for South would not have bid the slam holding two heart losers as well as a spade loser; there was no chance of a diamond trick; a count of spades showed South void there. So West rightly concentrated on making a trump trick.

His first thought was to lead a low spade, hoping that his partner would be able to uppercut with the club jack and promote a trick for the queen. As the cards lie this defence would have succeeded.

Alas, West had a second thought. If, he mused, *South* held the club jack—as was probable, on the basis of his jump to slam—passive defence was likely to succeed: South would no doubt finesse the clubs through East, reasoning that East had to have the queen for his opening bid, and lose to West's queen. So West switched to a passive heart.

South won with the heart ace, drew trumps, and claimed his slam. Too late, West had a third thought. He could have given himself an extra chance by leading the spade queen at the second trick. That would have established the spade jack as a trick in dummy, of course, but South could have no useful discard on it anyway. As the cards lie, East would then have ruffed his partner's spade queen with the club jack, knowing that this play could not hurt the defence—if South had a spade the ruff would still take the trick—and might help.

There was a subtle advantage in leading the spade queen rather than a low spade: East would not be tempted to ruff his partner's winner if he had a worthless trump holding. West's switch to a heart had been based on the fear that his partner would ruff a low spade with a low trump, in which case South would overruff and draw the three missing trumps with his ace-king.

As it turned out, the result was flat. When the German players later held the North-South cards they bid to six diamonds, which could not be defeated. It is quite curious that six clubs can fail with nine trumps in the combined hands, while six diamonds, with only seven trumps, is unbeatable.

Improbable Attack Can Embarrass a Sleepy Defence

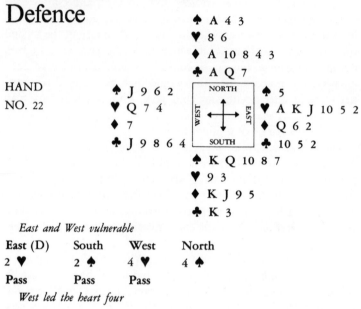

HAND NO. 22

```
              ♠ A 4 3
              ♥ 8 6
              ♦ A 10 8 4 3
              ♣ A Q 7

♠ J 9 6 2      NORTH      ♠ 5
♥ Q 7 4    WEST    EAST   ♥ A K J 10 5 2
♦ 7                       ♦ Q 6 2
♣ J 9 8 6 4    SOUTH      ♣ 10 5 2

              ♠ K Q 10 8 7
              ♥ 9 3
              ♦ K J 9 5
              ♣ K 3
```

East and West vulnerable

East (D)	South	West	North
2 ♥	2 ♠	4 ♥	4 ♠
Pass	Pass	Pass	

West led the heart four

Some years back a cautious New Yorker refused to enter an elevator in the Empire State Building. He was afraid, he explained, that something might happen to the elevator if an aeroplane hit the side of the building. Everyone laughed at him, but a week or so later that strange accident did occur. He had the last laugh, for he had proved that one should not confuse the improbable with the impossible.

It is a lesson that bridge-players need to learn also. Consider a position such as this in the trump suit:

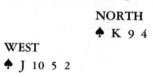

```
            NORTH
            ♠ K 9 4
   WEST
   ♠ J 10 5 2
```

If the declarer leads a low card from his hand, it is normal for West to play low: playing an honour is a fatal error if East has a singleton or doubleton queen. West knows that in theory he could lose a trick by playing low, but he also knows that in practice South will not finesse the nine if he has both ace and queen. Such a play would flout the percentages, but it might just happen. South might have reason to suspect that West has four cards in the suit, and he could have more positive motivation if West is a player who carelessly holds his cards so that his opponents can see them.

The diagrammed deal shows a similar situation. In a match conducted in Paris to determine the 1969 French team for the World Championship, West permitted himself to make a play which could not gain. He felt sure that it could not lose either, but events proved he was wrong.

East's opening bid of two hearts was a weak two-bid, and South overcalled with two spades. West's jump to four hearts was a tactical move based on three-card trump support, a single-ton, and a generous measure of optimism. He may have hoped to intimidate North-South, but North had the best hand at the table and had no hesitation in going to four spades. At this vulnerability East-West were not tempted to go further: they would have been down at least 800 points in five hearts doubled.

East's hearts won the first two tricks against four spades, and he switched to a club, his safest play. South took the club king followed by the ace and queen in dummy. He discarded a diamond from his hand and led to the spade king.

His next lead was the spade seven, an innocent-seeming card which trapped West into playing low. West knew, of course, that he could make sure of a trump trick by playing his nine, but he also 'knew' that South was going to play the ace from the dummy.

But to West's dismay and embarrassment, South played low from the dummy and the seven won the trick. A spade was led to the ace, and South worked out that West was likely to be short in diamonds. He finessed the diamond jack because he needed a quick entry to his hand, and made an overtrick by drawing the last trump.

South's strange play in the trump suit had reason behind it.

He judged from the bidding that the side-suits were unlikely to break, and he assumed provisionally that East was short in spades. If East had held a doubleton spade originally, the duck in spades would have lost a trick but not the contract. East would have been endplayed: a diamond lead would have solved South's problem in that suit, and any other lead would have allowed the declarer to discard another diamond from his hand and ruff in the dummy.

At the worst, East would have been able to win the trump lead and play a third trump. South would then have had a good count on the hand. Playing East for six hearts, three clubs and three spades he would be able to judge the diamond position to avoid the loss of a trick.

West had some consolation in facing up to post-mortem jeers of players and kibitzers who asked him how he had managed to lose a certain trump trick. South would have made his contract in any event, once he located four trumps in the West hand. He would have played West to be short in diamonds to justify his jump to four hearts.

West has now learned his lesson and keeps a wary eye open for plays that just seem to be impossible.

Sink Me the Ship, Master Player

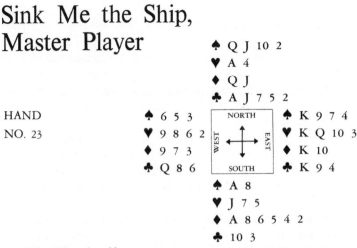

```
                              ♠ Q J 10 2
                              ♥ A 4
                              ♦ Q J
                              ♣ A J 7 5 2
HAND          ♠ 6 5 3          NORTH          ♠ K 9 7 4
NO. 23        ♥ 9 8 6 2                        ♥ K Q 10 3
              ♦ 9 7 3    WEST  ←→  EAST        ♦ K 10
              ♣ Q 8 6          SOUTH           ♣ K 9 4
                              ♠ A 8
                              ♥ J 7 5
                              ♦ A 8 6 5 4 2
                              ♣ 10 3
```

Neither side vulnerable

South(D)	West	North	East
Pass	Pass	1 ♣	Dbl.
2 NT	Pass	3 NT	Pass
Pass	Pass		

West led the heart two

Note: Recommended bid for South, British style, would be two diamonds, not 2 NT, which would show full values for a three club limit raise.

The Merrimack is famous historically not only for being one of the participants in the first naval battle between armour-plated vessels but also for having been scuttled twice, once by the Union forces and later by the Confederates. This association provides the name for a rare defensive manoeuvre at the bridge table.

The Merrimack Coup is the deliberate sacrifice of an important card aimed at depriving the declarer of a vital entry. This usually develops when the dummy has a long suit about to be established and a side entry which can be attacked.

When the crucial entry is in the closed hand, the coup is very difficult indeed to spot in actual play. A fine example occurred on the diagrammed deal, played at the 'Bridge House' in New York.

North opened in third position with one club, and East doubled in the hope of finding his partner with a major suit. South's hand did not seem right for a redouble and was too strong for a bid of one diamond, so he made an unusual tactical jump to two no-trumps. In tournament play this rare bid would suggest a hand with about 10 points and a club fit, but this was a rubber bridge game and South had a simple aim: he wanted to play the hand.

North raised to three no-trumps, grumbling that he was never permitted to play a hand, and West led the heart two. South ducked in dummy, and East won with the queen. He returned the heart three to drive out the ace in dummy, and South faced the problem of developing nine tricks.

The only hope was to develop the diamond suit, which offered a chance of making five diamond tricks, two spades and two other aces. South therefore led the diamond queen, and East correctly covered with the king.

South could not afford to play the diamond ace at this stage, and he could hardly avoid the loss of a diamond trick. He, therefore, ducked, and East cashed his two remaining heart tricks. The position was then:

```
                    NORTH
                    ♠ Q J 10 2
                    ♥ -
                    ♦ J
WEST                ♣ A J 7              EAST
♠ 6 5 3                                  ♠ K 9 7 4
♥ -                                      ♥ -
♦ 9 7                                    ♦ 10
♣ Q 8 6             SOUTH                ♣ K 9 4
                    ♠ A 8
                    ♥ -
                    ♦ A 8 6 5 4
                    ♣ 10
```

The East cards were held by Victor Shen, a well-known New York expert, and he studied the situation carefully. He saw that South might be able to make his contract if he held a long diamond suit and the spade ace, a likely circumstance.

On this analysis, East found the only play to defeat the contract: the spade king. This drove the spade ace from the South hand before the declarer had an opportunity to unblock the diamonds. East thus generously gave South two extra spade tricks, but now the declarer could only make one diamond trick instead of the five he had hoped for.

West congratulated East upon his defence, and East thanked West for holding the diamond nine, the card that prevented South from overtaking his diamond jack.

North, a Scotsman, had two complaints.

'If ye'd let me play the hand, I'd have made that contract,' he pointed out to South. 'The lead would have been the king of hearts.

'And why does Shen have to play against me when he chooses to mak' merry wi' his Merrimack?'

Don't Fall Asleep With a Yarborough

HAND
NO. 24

North
- ♠ A 7 4
- ♥ A 9 8 7
- ♦ 5 3
- ♣ J 9 7 2

West
- ♠ K Q 10
- ♥ 4
- ♦ K J 10 6 2
- ♣ A K 10 6

East
- ♠ 8 3
- ♥ J 10 6 2
- ♦ 9 7 4
- ♣ 8 5 4 3

South
- ♠ J 9 6 5 2
- ♥ K Q 5 3
- ♦ A Q 8
- ♣ Q

Both sides vulnerable

West (D)	North	East	South
1 ♦	Pass	Pass	1 ♠
Pass	2 ♣	Pass	3 ♦
Pass	3 ♥	Pass	4 ♠
Pass	Pass	Pass	

West led the club king

Perhaps it is an ingrained horror of poverty that causes many players to go into mental retirement when they find themselves with a virtually worthless hand, but someone with a near-yarborough may still have a vital role to play in the bidding or the play.

In the diagrammed deal, played in the quarter-final round of the Vanderbilt Knockout Team Championship in Cleveland in 1969, East thought he could fall asleep after registering a determination to hang on to his hearts. He was wrong.

Both teams climbed up to game, but one of them was out of luck; a four-one trump break wrecked South's slim chances of making four hearts, and he was down two.

When the South cards were held by Jim Cayne, one of New York's top-ranked experts, he made a protective bid of one spade after West's opening one diamond bid had been passed by

East. When his partner supported spades, he invited game with a cue bid of three diamonds.

When North then bid three hearts, South considered supporting the suit but chose to bid four spades in order to prevent a diamond lead from East through his ace-queen.

West led the club king against four spades, and switched to the spade king at the second trick. He had a problem when South ducked, and did the best he could by switching to his singleton heart. Dummy's seven was covered by the ten and king, and South led to the spade ace in dummy.

As West was known to have begun with the king-queen of spades, the ace-king of clubs and had bid diamonds, South judged the heart situation accurately. He led the heart eight and let it run, keeping the ace in dummy as a possible entry.

West was reluctant to have the lead, so he refused to ruff, and refused again when South led to the heart queen. Then the position was:

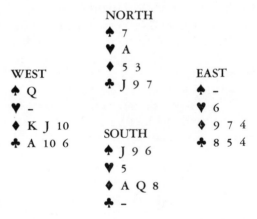

```
                    NORTH
                    ♠ 7
                    ♥ A
                    ♦ 5 3
   WEST             ♣ J 9 7        EAST
   ♠ Q                             ♠ -
   ♥ -                             ♥ 6
   ♦ K J 10                        ♦ 9 7 4
   ♣ A 10 6         SOUTH          ♣ 8 5 4
                    ♠ J 9 6
                    ♥ 5
                    ♦ A Q 8
                    ♣ -
```

A trump lead forced West to win, and East, who had lost interest in the proceedings, made a vital contribution—to South. In the belief that his hand was useless, he discarded the diamond four. His idea was to advise his partner that he held nothing of value in diamonds, a message that was not quite accurate and hardly needed sending.

South needed all the remaining tricks at this point, and thanks to East's co-operation, he was in a position to take them.

If West had returned the club ace, South would have ruffed, cashed his last trump, discarding a diamond from dummy, and led a heart. West would have been forced to unguard the diamond king or the club ten, and declarer would take the rest of the tricks.

A switch to a low club would have been no better. South would have won with the nine in dummy, discarding a diamond from his hand. He would have then ruffed a club, and led his last trump.

This play would force West to discard a diamond, and his last three cards would be the king-jack of diamonds and the club ace. He would be unable to stand the pressure when South led his last heart to dummy's ace at the 11th trick.

West did the best he could by leading the diamond jack, surrendering a trick in that suit rather than in clubs. South won with the queen and led his last two trumps. West parted with two clubs safely, but was squeezed in the minor suits when South led to the heart ace at the 11th trick.

Notice the difference if East does not discard his diamond four. At the 11th trick West can safely discard a diamond honour, and East's diamond nine prevents South from making a trick with the eight.

West was irritated at being endplayed and then squeezed in the same hand, and spoke sharply to his partner: 'Just because you have a poor hand,' he told East, 'you don't have to be a poor defender.'

Beware Signals That Tell Too Much

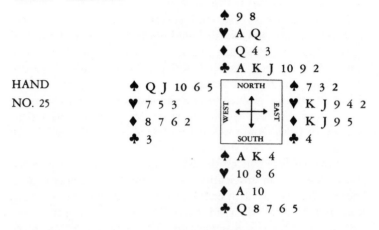

♠ 9 8
♥ A Q
♦ Q 4 3
♣ A K J 10 9 2

HAND
NO. 25

♠ Q J 10 6 5
♥ 7 5 3
♦ 8 7 6 2
♣ 3

NORTH
WEST   EAST
SOUTH

♠ 7 3 2
♥ K J 9 4 2
♦ K J 9 5
♣ 4

♠ A K 4
♥ 10 8 6
♦ A 10
♣ Q 8 7 6 5

North and South vulnerable, with a part-score of 40

South (D)	West	North	East
1 ♣	Pass	6 ♣	Pass
Pass	Pass		

West led the spade queen

Unlike Generals and quarterbacks, bridge players cannot use codes to transmit important instructions. Any signals sent by one defender to another will give information to an alert declarer, so the defender must feel sure that his partner needs help to conduct a successful defence.

The routine discard of a high card to show strength in a suit is used far too often by average players. Nine times out of ten such a signal is superfluous, either because partner has no significant part to play, or because he can work out what to do without help.

Such signals are very likely to tip off the declarer and allow him to find the winning line of play. The diagrammed deal, played at the Cavendish Club in New York, is an awful warning against signalling to the benefit of the declarer.

The bidding was brief and spectacular. After South had opened with one club, North found himself unable to think of a sensible bid. In normal circumstances an expert would probably choose between one diamond and two hearts, without feeling enthusiastic about either action.

In this case the problem was complicated by the part-score of 40. A jump to three clubs was ruled out, because this bid is enough for game. South would be likely to pass in the belief that his partner held a rather weaker hand.

North took the bull by the horns and jumped directly to six clubs. This was an unscientific gamble, but not an unreasonable one: the fate of the slam could easily depend upon the opening lead, and the direct slam bid leaves West very much in the dark.

South was Barbara Kachmar of New York, one of the most talented woman players in the game. She studied her prospects after West had led the queen of spades, and decided that the heart king needed to be on her left.

However, she had second thoughts at the third trick. She won with the spade ace, led to the club ace and returned to the club queen. At this point East triumphantly discarded the heart nine, eager to give his partner the news that the heart finesse would fail. This information was of no value to West, but was of considerable interest to South.

On the next club lead East continued on his revealing path by throwing the diamond nine. South now had a good idea that the missing red-suit honours were all on her right, but it was not clear how this knowledge could be utilised.

South knew that she could establish a diamond trick by leading towards the ace-ten, but that was not going to help. Instead she cashed the spade king, ruffed a spade in the dummy, and led another round of trumps. The position was then as opposite.

South led her last trump, and East suddenly found himself in trouble. He threw a heart, and South promptly played the ace of hearts followed by the queen. East had to lead from the diamond king, and the heart ten was declarer's 12th trick.

NORTH
♠ –
♥ A Q
♦ Q 4 3
♣ J

WEST
♠ J
♥ 7 5 3
♦ 8 7
♣ –

EAST
♠ –
♥ K J 9
♦ K J 9
♣ –

SOUTH
♠ –
♥ 10 8 6
♦ A 10
♣ 8

East would have been no better off if he had discarded a diamond. He would then have been endplayed by the lead of the diamond ace followed by the ten.

South was duly grateful to East for his share in bringing about this rare criss-cross endplay. 'Decent of you to discard those nines,' she observed.

'That all depends which side you're on,' grumbled West. 'I thought it was indecent.'

Second Hand Low . . .
and Low . . .
and Low

HAND

NO. 26

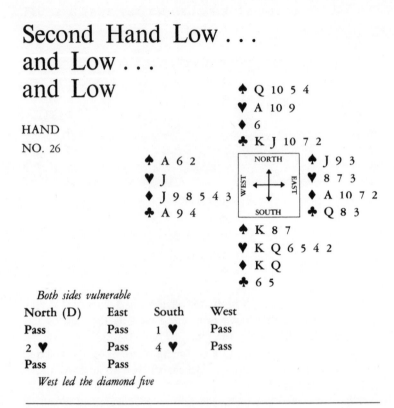

♠ Q 10 5 4
♥ A 10 9
♦ 6
♣ K J 10 7 2

♠ A 6 2
♥ J
♦ J 9 8 5 4 3
♣ A 9 4

♠ J 9 3
♥ 8 7 3
♦ A 10 7 2
♣ Q 8 3

♠ K 8 7
♥ K Q 6 5 4 2
♦ K Q
♣ 6 5

Both sides vulnerable

North (D)	East	South	West
Pass	Pass	1 ♥	Pass
2 ♥	Pass	4 ♥	Pass
Pass	Pass		

West led the diamond five

Second-hand low is an old whist maxim with fewer exceptions than most bridge rules of thumb. Nevertheless the inexperienced player finds it difficult to resist the temptation to climb up with an ace to make sure of a trick. In most cases it is not only right to duck, but important to duck without any revealing hesitation. The defender must plan his tactics in advance so that he makes his play smoothly when the declarer attacks the crucial suit. In the diagrammed deal, played in a Reisinger Knockout Team Championship match, West had to resist playing high not once but three times, each time nonchalantly. And it worked.

The obvious contract of four hearts could be reached in many ways. North has a wide choice of responses in standard methods after he has passed and South has opened one heart: one spade, two clubs, a jump to three hearts or even three clubs. South is not obliged to rebid, so a simple black suit response carries a danger that the bidding will end before the right contract is found. A jump to three hearts normally indicates four-card support, but has much to recommend it in this case.

The bidding shown here followed the Roth-Stone system, in which a direct raise of a major suit is 'constructive', indicating a hand not far short of the values for an opening. So South jumped to game.

West led a diamond against four hearts, and when East won with the ace he returned a trump. South let this ride around to dummy's ace, picking up West's jack, and returned another heart to the king in his hand.

Now South had to plan carefully. He knew there were two more aces out against him which were sure winners for the defence. The problem, therefore, was to guess the clubs, and this was virtually a 50-50 proposition. The fact that East had already produced the diamond ace slightly suggested that the club ace would be with West, so South decided to lead to dummy's king.

West here began his careful ducking plays that were in the end to provide a brilliant defence and give declarer a chance to fail. He played the four and let dummy win with the king.

South then led a low club from the dummy, hoping to stick West in with his ace and thus endplaying him: any return from West would have given South his crucial 10th trick. But Ross Dorfman of New York sitting East did not make the routine play of the club eight. He alertly put up the club queen, winning the trick and protecting his partner from the endplay. East had no lead problem, for he had a trump to play.

South won the trump trick in dummy with the ten and then ruffed a club, forcing West's ace to fall and establishing dummy's clubs. But West, John Solodar of New York, was not discouraged and not inclined to give up his second-hand-low strategy. He simply realised he would have to follow his earlier duck in clubs with two ducks in spades.

South, trying to set up an entry in the dummy in order to cash his clubs, then led the spade king, hoping it would be overtaken by the ace and make dummy's queen good. But West played low without hesitation. South continued with a spade—and West made another nonchalant duck.

Now South had to stop and guess: Where are the spade ace and the spade jack? Well, he guessed, East must have the ace and West the jack. He played the spade ten from dummy which lost to the jack and he was down one. West's shrewd ducking had kept South from ever knowing how the spades were sitting and thus led him into error.

It is interesting to note that there is really a better play for the hand than South made here—though, as the cards lie, it also goes down one. As soon as he is on lead, South should immediately finesse the club jack. The reason is that if this play wins, the clubs set up and the contract is a virtual certainty. Any other play, such as leading directly to the king of clubs, does nothing to solve the spade problem and it is still possible to lose two tricks there—as we saw above. That is, providing there's a good second-hand-low man playing West.

Duck Without Hesitation—
but Hesitate
to Duck

HAND
NO. 27

```
                 ♠ 7 4
                 ♥ J 2
                 ♦ A 10 9
                 ♣ A K Q 9 7 3
♠ A 9 5 2    NORTH      ♠ Q 10 8 6
♥ 10 4    WEST    EAST  ♥ Q 9 8 3
♦ 8 7 6 3              ♦ J 5 4 2
♣ 8 6 2      SOUTH      ♣ 5
                 ♠ K J 3
                 ♥ A K 7 6 5
                 ♦ K Q
                 ♣ J 10 4
```

Both sides vulnerable

South (D)	West	North	East
1 NT	Pass	6 NT	Pass
Pass	Pass		

West led the diamond eight

Ducking plays often need to be made without any revealing hesitation. Consider this common situation:

```
        ♠ K Q 10
        Dummy
        ♠ 5 4 3
        Declarer
```

The declarer leads to the king-queen in dummy and hopes someone will take the ace. If the ace appears on his right he finesses the ten next time. But good defenders will refuse to win the ace immediately and as long as the ducking is performed smoothly South will have no clue as to what to do when leading low towards dummy later.

The declarer has a much better chance when the situation is reversed and the honours are in the closed hand, for then the left-hand defender will be reluctant to duck a king, not knowing who has the queen. Nevertheless, an expert defender will sometimes refuse to take the king with the ace in such circumstances, realising that if the contract is in no-trumps an early lead to the king in the closed hand is unlikely unless the declarer has the queen in support.

There was no king-queen-ten combination in the diagrammed deal, played in the Eastern Regional Championships, but it was the possibility of such a holding that determined the fate of South's slam contract. South was an expert, and he had a famous star on his left, a factor which had a bearing on the play.

Most players would bid one heart, but there is something to be said for bidding one no-trump on occasions with a five-card heart suit. If South had bid one heart in this case he would have been faced with an unsatisfactory rebid after a response of one spade.

North made a sensible direct bid of six no-trumps. He was willing to give up the possibility that six clubs was the best contract, partly because he wanted the opening lead to come to South's major-suit holdings and partly because of the match-point advantage of playing no-trumps rather than clubs.

West felt no temptation to lead the spade ace, which would have given South his 12th trick immediately, since this is hardly ever good policy against a no-trump slam. Instead he selected the diamond eight as his safest lead, and South won in his hand with the king, East playing low. South counted 11 top tricks, and saw that the spade suit offered the only substantial chance of a 12th.

There were two good reasons for tackling the spades as quickly as possible. First, an immediate spade play might discourage the defenders from continuing a suit the declarer seems to favour and thus make it difficult for them to take a second spade trick. Second, South could not afford to cash diamonds at once, which would establish tricks for the defence when it got in, or even clubs, which would cut his own communications.

South saw that to get his extra spade trick he would have to find either the ace or the queen on his right, and the chances were mathematically equal: West was just as likely to have the ace and not the queen as the queen and not the ace. He took a chance that East had the ace and at the second trick entered dummy with a club and led a spade to his king.

As the cards lay, this was the wrong decision and the defence was in a position to take two spade tricks immediately to defeat the contract. But this did not happen—West, the famous star, was a bit too clever. He refused to win the spade king with the ace, and refused without the slightest hesitation. He reasoned that South held the king-queen-ten combination discussed at the beginning of this commentary—especially since South had led the suit—and that his ace would be good any time. He hoped that the duck would lure South into believing that East held the ace and so would lead to his queen later.

As it happened South had had quite enough of the spade suit and had no intention of playing it again. He ran 12 tricks, actually making an overtrick when East unwisely parted with two hearts. The expert West was hoist on the petard of his own expert defence.

Notice that even if West had taken the spade king with the ace it is not certain he would have defeated the contract. Any return but a spade would have given South a chance to cash his winners and squeeze East in the major suits.

Slam Problems

Defenders: Look Twice Before Ruffing

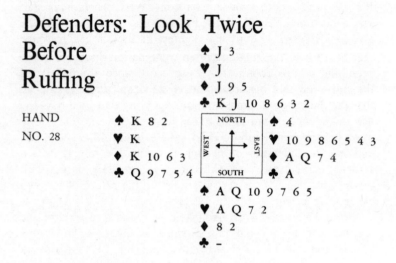

HAND NO. 28

```
                    ♠ J 3
                    ♥ J
                    ♦ J 9 5
                    ♣ K J 10 8 6 3 2
♠ K 8 2            NORTH            ♠ 4
♥ K          WEST        EAST       ♥ 10 9 8 6 5 4 3
♦ K 10 6 3                          ♦ A Q 7 4
♣ Q 9 7 5 4        SOUTH            ♣ A
                    ♠ A Q 10 9 7 6 5
                    ♥ A Q 7 2
                    ♦ 8 2
                    ♣ -
```

East and West vulnerable

West (D)	North	East	South
Pass	3 ♣	3 ♥	3 ♠
Pass	4 ♠	Pass	Pass
Dbl.	Pass	Pass	Pass

West led the heart king

A defender who unthinkingly ruffs his opponent's losing trick should beware: he may end up being a loser himself. When the declarer leads a loser from his own hand or the dummy, it is generally a mistake to ruff it, as was amply demonstrated in the diagrammed deal from the 1968 International Team Trials in Atlantic City, N.J. Two great players squandered the spade eight in the West position—and wound up with red faces in the post-mortem.

Six of the eight North-South pairs wound up in a spade contract. One East made four hearts doubled, which could not be defeated when played carefully; another East went down two in five hearts doubled after South led the ace and queen of spades, then shrewdly refused to take the heart king when it was led from the dummy, and finally ruffed when East made the mistake of trying to reach his hand with a club.

One North-South had the luck to be doubled in three spades, which could not be defeated. All the others were in four spades, and almost all were doubled. A typical auction is shown in the diagram. North pre-empted with three clubs, and East overcalled three hearts. South's bid of three spades was forcing, and North bid game knowing that South would not bid a suit of fewer than six cards.

West doubled on principle, judging that his partner had to have some strength for a vulnerable overcall at the three level and that the heart misfit would favour the defence. But general strength is not the best basis for doubling a voluntarily bid game contract, and defending four spades proved a tough chore.

At every table West led his singleton king of hearts and South won with the ace. One South ran into trouble by trying to cash the heart queen immediately. This would have been good play if West had had to follow suit. Instead he ruffed with the eight of spades, and South went wrong again by discarding a diamond from dummy. Had he overruffed with dummy's spade jack, he could have held his loss to a one-trick defeat by crossruffing. As it was, the defence took the king and ace of diamonds, a trump, a heart and the initial ruff to beat the contract two tricks.

At the other tables South led a low heart at the second trick. Charles Peres of Chicago simply discarded a club and awaited developments. South ruffed in the dummy, ruffed a club and ruffed his remaining small heart. The club king was no use to him, because when East's ace fell it was clear he was in a position to ruff the second round of clubs, so South's vision of success was shattered. West eventually gained the lead with the spade king, put his partner in with a diamond lead and then ruffed the declarer's heart queen when East returned that suit.

The excitement developed at two tables where players of world stature made a slight slip with the West cards. They both ruffed with the spade eight when South led a low heart at the second trick, and dummy overruffed. A low club was ruffed, removing East's ace. The position now was:

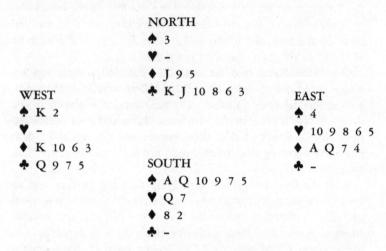

NORTH
♠ 3
♥ -
♦ J 9 5
♣ K J 10 8 6 3

WEST
♠ K 2
♥ -
♦ K 10 6 3
♣ Q 9 7 5

EAST
♠ 4
♥ 10 9 8 6 5
♦ A Q 7 4
♣ -

SOUTH
♠ A Q 10 9 7 5
♥ Q 7
♦ 8 2
♣ -

When South led the heart seven West was in a quandary. To ruff with the two would obviously be fatal: South would overruff in dummy, lead the club king and overruff East. The spade ace would then draw the singleton king and an overtrick would materialise. Discarding is no better. South would ruff in dummy, play the club king, and eventually lose only one trump trick and two diamonds.

West, therefore, ruffed with the spade king and led the spade two. The two South players at these tables, Dan Morse of Houston and Milton Rosenberg of Chicago, then had the rare pleasure of winning the first trump trick with the five. They claimed 10 tricks, conceding two diamonds.

The Play's the Thing
by which to Guess
the Queen

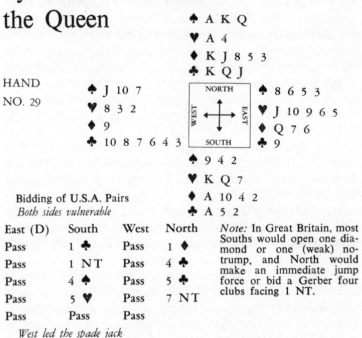

♠ A K Q
♥ A 4
♦ K J 8 5 3
♣ K Q J

HAND
NO. 29

WEST
♠ J 10 7
♥ 8 3 2
♦ 9
♣ 10 8 7 6 4 3

NORTH

EAST
♠ 8 6 5 3
♥ J 10 9 6 5
♦ Q 7 6
♣ 9

SOUTH
♠ 9 4 2
♥ K Q 7
♦ A 10 4 2
♣ A 5 2

Bidding of U.S.A. Pairs
Both sides vulnerable

East (D)	South	West	North
Pass	1 ♣	Pass	1 ♦
Pass	1 N T	Pass	4 ♣
Pass	4 ♠	Pass	5 ♣
Pass	5 ♥	Pass	7 N T
Pass	Pass	Pass	

West led the spade jack

Note: In Great Britain, most Souths would open one diamond or one (weak) no-trump, and North would make an immediate jump force or bid a Gerber four clubs facing 1 NT.

An old lady once complained that the experts are lucky because they always guess right. This was, of course, an exaggeration, but it is true that an expert will emerge successfully from guessing situations far more often than the average player.

When forced to guess the location of a queen, for example, as in the diamond situation shown in the diagram, the experienced player will search diligently for clues as to the position of the high cards and the distribution of the hand.

Sometimes the bidding will mark a particular defender with high-card strength, and sometimes the play will reveal that one defender is more likely to have length in the crucial suit. On rare occasions, as in the diagrammed deal played in the World Team

Olympiad in Deauville, France, the declarer can plan the play with the clear-cut aim of uncovering the opposing distribution.

Arthur Robinson of Philadelphia opened the South hand with one club and rebid one no-trump to show a minimum balanced hand. His partner, Robert Jordan, followed his quiet response of one diamond by forcing the bidding to the slam level with his jump to four clubs. That was the Gerber Convention, which many tournament players use as a substitute for Blackwood when the bid immediately preceding it is one no-trump or two no-trumps. South's bid of four spades showed two aces (four diamonds = no aces, four hearts = one ace, etc.), and North's five clubs asked for kings.

When South indicated he had two kings, North could then count 10 top tricks: three in spades and clubs, two in hearts and diamonds. There was no way to find out where the red queens were—especially the diamond queen—but North saw that there was a good chance for his diamonds to run and took the reasonable plunge to seven no-trumps. The odds were good enough: grand slams should be bid more readily in match play than in rubber bridge.

In leading against a seven contract the prime consideration is to avoid conceding a trick with the lead, so West led the spade jack. Robinson won in the dummy and studied his prospects. There were nine sure tricks, and no more, outside the diamond suit, and South decided to use them to elicit whatever information he could. He decided to postpone the diamond decision as long as possible.

South cashed three spade winners in dummy and noted that both players followed each time. He cashed his three heart tricks and again both players followed. The club ace was played, followed by a club to the king—revealing the delightful news that East had begun life with only one club.

Now South did a simple calculation. He knew that West had begun with exactly six clubs and at least three cards in each major suit. That left room for at most one diamond with West, so the declarer knew he could take the finesse through East. He led the diamond king from dummy and when both defenders followed he finessed his diamond ten with complete assurance. When the ten won the grand slam was claimed.

The Swiss players with the North-South cards bid only to six no-trumps, which was certainly not wrong This contract was made exactly, for the declarer took the sure way of making it by taking the ace and king of diamonds immediately and then giving up a trick to the queen, giving him twelve sure tricks.

Players who are faced with a two-way guess for a missing queen have been known to attempt non-technical solutions in the absence of legitimate inferences from the bidding and play. The late Hal Sims had a psychological method. He would brood on the problem for several minutes until one of the defenders broke the tension by lighting a cigarette or ordering a drink. He would then conclude this player held the crucial queen and was trying to hide his nervousness by a display of nonchalance. As the laws permit a player to draw inferences at his own risk from the behaviour of the opponents, the Sims system is apparently ethical.

Another method, which goes well beyond the borders of acceptable conduct, was used by a European player who would think for five minutes and then lead quickly from the wrong hand. It was a fair bet from his angle that the player who objected and was, therefore, interested in what was going on, held the crucial queen.

To Draw or Not to Draw— That Is the Question

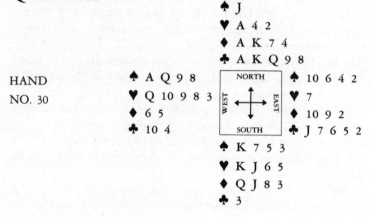

<table>
<tr><td></td><td></td><td>♠ J</td><td></td></tr>
<tr><td></td><td></td><td>♥ A 4 2</td><td></td></tr>
<tr><td></td><td></td><td>♦ A K 7 4</td><td></td></tr>
<tr><td></td><td></td><td>♣ A K Q 9 8</td><td></td></tr>
</table>

HAND
NO. 30

	NORTH	
♠ A Q 9 8		♠ 10 6 4 2
♥ Q 10 9 8 3	WEST ← → EAST	♥ 7
♦ 6 5		♦ 10 9 2
♣ 10 4	SOUTH	♣ J 7 6 5 2

♠ K 7 5 3
♥ K J 6 5
♦ Q J 8 3
♣ 3

East and West vulnerable

East (D)	South	West	North
Pass	Pass	Pass	1 ♣
Pass	1 ♦	Pass	2 ♥
Pass	4 ♥	Pass	4 NT
Pass	5 ♣	Pass	6 ♦
Pass	Pass	Pass	

West led the spade ace

Plenty of bridge players are said to be destitute because they failed to draw trumps promptly. But probably a greater number are in the same unhappy condition because they drew trumps too often. The basic rule is to draw trumps unless there is a prospect of ruffs in the shorter trump hand—usually the dummy —but as usual there are exceptions.

Whether or not to draw trumps can be a difficult decision even for an expert, as the diagrammed deal played in a New York exhibition match demonstrates. A world-famous player in the

South seat, suffering from fatigue, went down in a slam contract he would normally have made precisely because he made the wrong choice.

The bidding was good. North's hand was not quite worth a forcing opening, although that would have been justified if his suits had been majors instead of minors. South's bid of one diamond, based on the theory that a player with four-card suits should respond economically, worked out well. North's jump to two hearts was the only way in which he could show his enormous strength, and he planned to support diamonds later. As it turned out, the diamond fit was shown at the level of six after South had shown moderate strength by jumping to four hearts and North had used Blackwood.

Leading an ace against a slam is more often right than wrong, but it is dangerous to generalise. In this case West decided to lead the spade ace because North's bidding had strongly suggested a singleton spade and there seemed to be some danger in leading any other suit. As it turned out, however, the lead established South's king, a vital trick. A heart lead, in the faint hope that East would be able to ruff, would have been equally disastrous, but a club or a diamond would not have helped the declarer. A spade was continued and after winning with the king the declarer had a difficult planning problem. Was it right to draw trumps?

Assuming even breaks in both minor suits, South saw that the slam could be made by drawing trumps. After drawing them, he then cashed the club ace and ruffed a club, in the expectation that dummy's remaining club would be established. But when dummy was entered with the heart ace and the king and queen of clubs were led, East proved to have a stopper. South desperately ran to the heart suit, but West was in full control there and the slam failed.

In this case, there was a better play than drawing trumps, and in planning the play South should have tried this instead of depending on the even breaks. He should have led immediately to the club ace and ruffed a club. The risk of being overruffed by West at this stage would be negligible. The diamond queen would then be cashed, followed by a diamond to the king in dummy. South would now be in command.

With a normal 3-2 trump division, which in fact exists, South has no problem. He ruffs dummy's remaining low club with the diamond jack, crosses to the heart ace, draws the missing trump with the ace and claims the remaining tricks with top cards. He makes a total of six trump tricks, one spade, two hearts and three clubs.

Even with a 4-1 trump break, South has several chances. As soon as one defender shows out on the second round of trumps, he can lead a third round immediately to his jack, and return to the heart ace in dummy in order to draw the last opposing trump. He would then have 12 tricks with a normal 4-3 club division, and if that chance failed he could still fall back on finessing the heart jack for his 12th trick. Only if all suits broke badly to boot could South go down.

Interestingly enough, South still has a play for the contract even if he misses the correct line and instead draws all the trumps. As an elementary precaution against a possible 5-2 break in the clubs (as actually happened), he should have simply played the three top club honours from the dummy before taking his first ruff. This then would have showed him that West was void on the third round and, therefore, a ruffing finesse should be taken against East's jack. As the cards lie, this would make the slam.

What Good Is a Dummy If You Can't Get There?

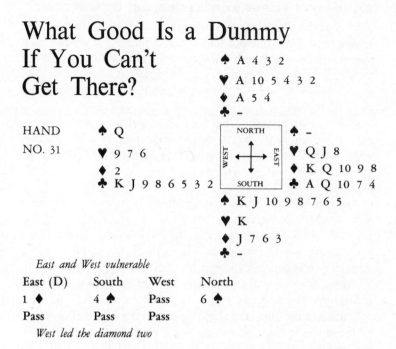

```
                          ♠ A 4 3 2
                          ♥ A 10 5 4 3 2
                          ♦ A 5 4
                          ♣ -
HAND      ♠ Q              NORTH          ♠ -
NO. 31    ♥ 9 7 6                          ♥ Q J 8
          ♦ 2          WEST ←→ EAST        ♦ K Q 10 9 8
          ♣ K J 9 8 6 5 3 2  SOUTH         ♣ A Q 10 7 4
                          ♠ K J 10 9 8 7 6 5
                          ♥ K
                          ♦ J 7 6 3
                          ♣ -
```

East and West vulnerable

East (D)	South	West	North
1 ♦	4 ♠	Pass	6 ♠
Pass	Pass	Pass	

West led the diamond two

Nothing is more frustrating for a declarer than having good tricks across the table in dummy and not being able to get enough entries to use them. Careful play—and sometimes spectacular play—is needed to preserve entries or even to make the opponents create them for you.

The diagrammed hand was prepared by a group of sadistic experts in a 1957 tournament precisely to teach other experts this lesson. The hand is remarkable in two ways: not only is a dummy with first-round control in all four suits and four-card trump support left with only one effective entry after the first trick, but the winning line of play shows a decidedly spectacular way to insure an extra entry.

East made a normal opening bid of one diamond, expecting to show his club suit on the next round. He did not of course anticipate that his next opportunity to bid clubs would be at the level of seven. South had an obvious pre-emptive overcall of four spades, and West did not feel inclined to bid his broken club suit at the five level with unfavourable vulnerability. North bid to the slam, since he held all the first-round controls and could expect South to make 12 tricks either by ruffing clubs or by establishing hearts.

(If West had chosen to bid his clubs and had wound up playing in a club slam, North would have needed a remarkable inspiration to keep West from making 11 tricks and thus to get the maximum penalty. He would have had to underlead his heart ace.)

An opening lead against six spades of a heart, a spade or a club would have solved all South's entry problems. He could play his top two hearts, then use the spade ace to reach dummy for a heart ruff to set up the suit, and finally go back to the dummy's diamond ace to cash his established winners. Result: 13 tricks. But West, of course, remembered his partner's opening bid and led the diamond two.

South had no trouble in deciding to win the first trick with the diamond ace in dummy, but finding a plan of play which could produce the required 12 tricks was another matter. His only hope was to establish dummy's hearts in order to discard the diamond losers from his hand. And even for this he had to assume that the hearts would be divided three-three, for with any other distribution he had no chance.

There is one possibility of endplaying West if he holds precisely Q J x of hearts. In that case South would cash the heart king, lead to the spade ace and cash the heart ace. On a heart lead from dummy a diamond would be discarded from the closed hand and West would find himself on play with nothing but clubs. The forced ruff-and-discard would allow South to reach the dummy to play heart winners.

But this method of play did not appeal to South, because it was likely that East held at least one heart honour as part of his opening bid. And it would not help him to find East with an honour, for West would then unblock the queen by throwing it under dummy's ace.

After some thought South found the right way. He hoped to make West give him the dummy entry he needed, and he reasoned it this way: West must be void in diamonds (the lead of the two has to be a singleton, rather than the lowest of three, since East had to have at least four diamonds for his bid), and he can have no more than one spade. If he can be thrown in, he will be forced to lead either a club—in which case South gets a ruff-and-discard—or a heart—in which case South discards a diamond loser on the ace.

So after taking the opening lead with dummy's diamond ace, South led back to his heart king and at the third trick led a low spade. West produced his singleton spade queen and was astonished when South played low from the dummy. Astonished, but not particularly delighted: he saw this remarkable ducking play gave South that essential extra entry to the dummy. Any way he played, the heart suit was established and the spade ace remained as the entry to cash the heart winners.

The experts who devised the deal pointed out that they could have increased the shock to West by giving him the spade six instead of the queen. But sadism had its limits.

Take It By and Large, 'Second-Hand Low' Is a First-Rate Rule

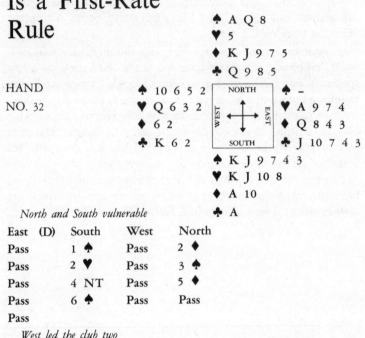

HAND NO. 32

♠ A Q 8
♥ 5
♦ K J 9 7 5
♣ Q 9 8 5

♠ 10 6 5 2
♥ Q 6 3 2
♦ 6 2
♣ K 6 2

♠ —
♥ A 9 7 4
♦ Q 8 4 3
♣ J 10 7 4 3

♠ K J 9 7 4 3
♥ K J 10 8
♦ A 10
♣ A

North and South vulnerable

East (D)	South	West	North
Pass	1 ♠	Pass	2 ♦
Pass	2 ♥	Pass	3 ♠
Pass	4 NT	Pass	5 ♦
Pass	6 ♠	Pass	Pass
Pass			

West led the club two

Perhaps the best of the rules of thumb which date back to the days of whist is 'second-hand low'. The exceptions are rather rare, and the player who looks for the exceptions is quite likely to get the worst of matters merely because he has looked.

NORTH
♥ K J 8 3

WEST
♥ A 9 5 4

Suppose you are sitting West, defending a contract of four spades. At an early stage the declarer leads the two from his hand, which is likely to be a singleton or a doubleton.

After a little thought you realise that the play of the ace might be right: if the declarer has a singleton, he may avoid the loss of a trick altogether if you play low. Against that, the play of the ace gives the declarer a certain trick with the king and rules out the chance that your partner will win the trick with the queen.

Unfortunately your 'little thought' is disastrous, because the declarer cannot now misguess. If you play low he will play the king, because your hesitation has betrayed your possession of the ace.

If you follow the second-hand-low rule automatically, you play low and the declarer will probably play the jack from the dummy. Now your partner can win with the queen—if he does not have it, the play will not matter—and your side has the upper hand. Either your side will make two tricks, or the declarer will be limited to one.

Players who know what to do in this situation often fall into the temptation of putting up the ace when the situation is reversed and a singleton is led from the dummy. The temptation to snatch an immediate trick is a strong one, but should be resisted.

If the declarer has, for example, Q J x in the suit, the play of the ace exposes partner's king to a ruffing finesse. If the declarer has K Q x, the play of the ace gives him two tricks when he can only make one after a duck.

The diagrammed deal shows the importance of playing second-hand-low without hesitating. In a match between the U.S. Aces of Dallas and a Californian team of stars, a contract of six spades was reached at both tables.

Don Krauss of Los Angeles, a former member of the United States international team, was the declarer after the orthodox bidding shown in the diagram, and the lead was the club two. He won with the ace, entered dummy by leading the diamond ten to the king, and played the heart five.

East was William Eisenberg of Dallas, a member of the 1969 international squad, and he played low on the heart lead without any revealing hesitation. Inevitably South misguessed by playing the jack. He knew that East might have played the ace if he held that card, so the ace was likely to be with West.

From this point South could not make the slam, although he

was still trying. He ruffed West's heart return in the dummy and led to the diamond ace. His plan was to ruff all his heart losers in the dummy, and this succeeded up to a point.

By the time he had ruffed the last two hearts and returned to his hand by ruffing clubs—clearly safer than ruffing diamonds—he was reduced to ♠ K J 9 7. He hoped the spade ten would fall singleton or doubleton, but West had that card thoroughly guarded and made the setting trick.

When the hand was replayed, North accidentally became the declarer in six spades after he had made an artificial control-showing response of one spade to a strong one club opening bid. The partnership was using a modified version of an Italian system.

East was, therefore, on lead, and played the heart ace, making it relatively easy for North to make the slam. East's choice of lead deprived him of a chance to match Eisenberg's faith in the principle of 'second-hand low'.

Sometimes it's the Count
That Counts Most

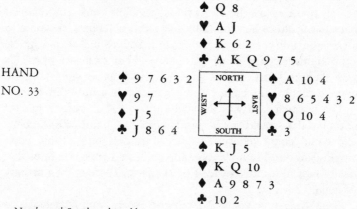

♠ Q 8
♥ A J
♦ K 6 2
♣ A K Q 9 7 5

HAND
NO. 33

♠ 9 7 6 3 2   ♠ A 10 4
♥ 9 7   ♥ 8 6 5 4 3 2
♦ J 5   ♦ Q 10 4
♣ J 8 6 4   ♣ 3

♠ K J 5
♥ K Q 10
♦ A 9 8 7 3
♣ 10 2

North and South vulnerable

West (D)	North	East	South
Pass	1 ♣	Pass	2 NT
Pass	4 ♣	Pass	4 ♥
Pass	6 NT	Pass	Pass
Pass			

Note: In American style 2 NT shows 13–15 points, not the 11–12 we would expect.

West led the spade three

Counting up to thirteen seems simple, and it helps to solve many difficult problems at the bridge table, both for the declarer and the defenders. But many players are not willing to make this effort, preferring to rely on intuition rather than calculation.

It is not always easy to spot the deals on which counting will pay a dividend. On the diagrammed deal from the Spring National Championships in Cleveland in 1969 nearly all the declarers failed to see the need to count and consequently failed in the contract.

At one table North opened one club on this powerful hand, on which two no-trumps was a possibility. The trick-taking potential of the club suit was sufficient compensation for the slight shortage of high-card points. South had the unbid suits well stopped and, therefore, preferred a jump to two no-trumps to the routine response of one diamond.

North's second-round four clubs was the Gerber convention, asking for aces on the Blackwood principle. Most tournament players use this when the four-club bid is a jump in response to a one no-trump or two no-trumps bid. South's bid of four hearts showed one ace, and North was happy to bid six no-trumps. This was likely to be at least as good a contract as six clubs, and the extra points for no-trumps were significant in a duplicate game.

The opening lead was the spade three, and East took his ace and played a second spade. South won in his hand with the king, and could count ten sure tricks. Most declarers at this point would lead out dummy's three top clubs and curse the fates that dealt West four clubs headed by the jack. There is then no way to make 12 tricks.

Gene Neiger, a young New York expert, rightly decided to postpone the decision in the club suit. The play of the spades strongly suggested that West held five cards originally, and he now sought out clues as to the distribution of the red suits.

The club ten was led to the queen in dummy, and three rounds of hearts were cashed. West discarded a spade, showing that he had started with a doubleton heart.

The next three tricks were taken with the king of diamonds, the ace of diamonds and the jack of spades. The position was:

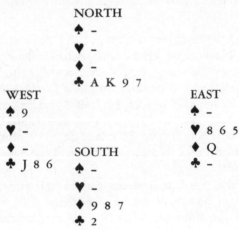

```
                    NORTH
                    ♠ -
                    ♥ -
                    ♦ -
                    ♣ A K 9 7
    WEST                            EAST
    ♠ 9                             ♠ -
    ♥ -                             ♥ 8 6 5
    ♦ -            SOUTH            ♦ Q
    ♣ J 8 6        ♠ -             ♣ -
                   ♥ -
                   ♦ 9 8 7
                   ♣ 2
```

At this point Neiger made his arithmetical effort and attempted to count the West hand. He was confident that West had started with five spades and two hearts and, therefore, that West had three cards remaining in the minor suits.

If West held the diamond queen and the club jack, any play of the club suit would succeed. So South assumed that West held the two missing small clubs, and one of the missing honours.

It seemed a toss-up whether West held the diamond queen or the club jack, but there was a rather subtle clue. If West had held both queen and jack of diamonds, he might well have false-carded with the queen in the hope of deceiving South about the distribution. His play of the jack on the second round suggested that he did not have the queen, so South placed him with the club jack and finessed dummy's nine.

When East showed out on the club play, South breathed a sigh of relief. He made a difficult slam, and earned a top score, by a combination of good reasoning and careful counting.

Keep Track of the Jack

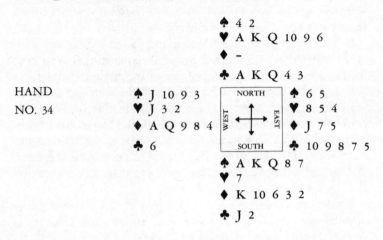

```
                              ♠ 4 2
                              ♥ A K Q 10 9 6
                              ♦ -
                              ♣ A K Q 4 3
HAND          ♠ J 10 9 3    NORTH      ♠ 6 5
NO. 34        ♥ J 3 2     WEST   EAST   ♥ 8 5 4
              ♦ A Q 9 8 4             ♦ J 7 5
              ♣ 6            SOUTH      ♣ 10 9 8 7 5
                              ♠ A K Q 8 7
                              ♥ 7
                              ♦ K 10 6 3 2
                              ♣ J 2
```

Both sides vulnerable

North (D)	East	South	West
2 ♥	Pass	2 ♠	Pass
3 ♣	Pass	3 ♦	Pass
3 ♥	Pass	3 ♠	Pass
5 ♠	Pass	6 ♠	Pass
Pass	Pass		

West led the spade jack

The solidity of the trump suit is often an important factor when
a slam bid is being considered. Several conventions in use in
tournament play tackle the problem of locating the ace, king
and queen of trumps, but science is of no help when it is a
question of a jack.

On the diagrammed deal, played in a practice class, North-
South had a wide choice of slam contracts—spades, hearts and
clubs were all possible at the six-level and the seven-level. In
each suit the jack was a crucial card: North was hesitant about
seven hearts because the heart jack might represent a trick for

the defence, and was similarly concerned about the club jack for the purposes of seven clubs.

North-South were using traditional strong two-bids, and North was fully justified in opening with two hearts. He had only 18 points in high cards, but points are not the crucial factor in this decision. The two-bidder must expect to be able to make a game if his partner's hand is worthless, and North fulfilled this requirement with something to spare. He had only two losers, and 11 probable winners.

South bid his hand strongly, but the bidding revealed a misfit. When South rebid the spades, North assumed that his partner held a strong six-card suit and that a spade contract would be as good as anything.

It was just as well for North that he did not know about the club jack, for he would have bid seven clubs and been defeated by the unlucky trump break. Instead he unselfishly—perhaps too unselfishly—allowed South to play in six spades.

If South had held the spade jack as well as the ace-king-queen, seven spades would have been an excellent contract. As it was, he needed a three-three trump division to make 13 tricks.

It seemed easy to make 12 tricks, but South would have been wise to plan his play more carefully. He should have expected a four-two break, which is much more likely than three-three when six cards are missing.

In practice South seized the opportunity to ruff a diamond in dummy. He won the first trick in his hand, ruffed a diamond, and re-entered his hand with a club lead to the jack. Two high trumps followed, leaving West with a trump winner.

South realised belatedly that his contract was in danger. He had four more diamonds to dispose of and these had to be discarded on dummy's winners. As it happened there was no way to achieve this, for after taking three rounds of hearts, and two discards, West was in a position to take the next two tricks however the declarer continued.

If West had held one more club and one fewer diamond, South would have had to guess whether to play a third round of hearts before a third round of clubs. West would have had the chance to lead the declarer along the wrong path by dropping the heart jack on the second round of the suit.

Many players would have gone down in the slam, just as South did. He made the common error of failing to think hard enough when the dummy appeared. The right play, an unusual one, was to allow West to win the first trick with the spade jack. Dummy still has a trump to deal with a diamond lead, and whatever West does his trumps can be drawn without difficulty.

South would have had to work harder if West had led his singleton club, which interferes with the declarer's communications. He can still succeed by winning in dummy and ducking a trump to West.

No West would consider underleading the diamond ace, but such a lead would probably have defeated the slam. South would have had to ruff two diamonds in dummy and guess the distribution exactly to make his contract.

A Case of the 'Ghoulies'

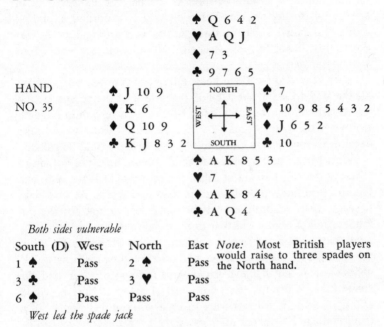

HAND
NO. 35

```
                        ♠ Q 6 4 2
                        ♥ A Q J
                        ♦ 7 3
                        ♣ 9 7 6 5
    ♠ J 10 9          NORTH          ♠ 7
    ♥ K 6       WEST  ←   →  EAST    ♥ 10 9 8 5 4 3 2
    ♦ Q 10 9                         ♦ J 6 5 2
    ♣ K J 8 3 2      SOUTH           ♣ 10
                        ♠ A K 8 5 3
                        ♥ 7
                        ♦ A K 8 4
                        ♣ A Q 4
```

Both sides vulnerable

South (D)	West	North	East
1 ♠	Pass	2 ♠	Pass
3 ♣	Pass	3 ♥	Pass
6 ♠	Pass	Pass	Pass

West led the spade jack

Note: Most British players would raise to three spades on the North hand.

The New Haven Railroad has always had a dedicated group of commuter bridge players: one of them once continued to commute after his retirement because he could not bear to miss his morning game. The brand of bridge is still the same—'Ghoulies', a variant in which the cards are never shuffled, and are dealt five at a time, five again, and finally three cards at the end.

This makes for freakish distribution and wild bidding. In the play of the hand great care is required, for it is not uncommon to find all suits breaking badly and winning honours falling to defenders' ruffs. A quick-thinking commuter, even when subject to timetable time pressure, can often devise unusual manoeuvres in the play to allow for distributional hazards. This was the case recently in the diagrammed deal, played by Don Stern of Larchmont, N.Y., the editor of my book, *The New York Times Guide to Practical Bridge.*

South's hand was almost worth an opening forcing bid, and he had hopes of a slam as soon as his partner showed a fit in spades by raising to two. Three clubs was a normal exploring move, but North's bid of three hearts was ambiguous. It was apparently meant to show strength, but most players would consider it showed length.

South regarded the three-heart bid as encouraging and jumped all the way to slam. West made the safe lead of the spade jack and South studied his prospects. He saw that he would have no trouble if the spades broke 2-2, for dummy's hearts would take care of his club losers and the diamond losers would be ruffed.

But if he ran into a three-one spade break, he could not afford to draw the third spade at once, for that would leave only one trump in dummy to deal with the diamond losers. At first sight it seems risky to draw even two rounds of trumps, for the defenders might lead a third trump on gaining the lead with the heart king. But South had a solution to this problem: the lie of the spades could determine the method of playing the hearts.

South won the first two tricks with the spade queen and the spade king, and noted East's discard of a heart. Now he could afford to concede a heart trick to East without any danger of a trump return. He, therefore, finessed the heart queen successfully.

If it had been West who had shown out on the second spade, the heart play would have been the ace followed by the queen, discarding unless East covered with the king.

When the heart queen won, South adopted a line of play which guaranteed the slam against any distribution of the defenders' cards. He took two high diamonds and ruffed a diamond in dummy. Next the heart ace was cashed, and as it happened the king fell from West and everything was easy. Both club losers were discarded, and West was welcome to make his trump.

The fall of the heart king from West was not in the least necessary for the success of South's plan. If West had followed with a low heart, the heart jack would have been ruffed and the last diamond led. If West had then ruffed, he would have been endplayed, with the choice of leading a club to the ace-queen or conceding a ruff-and-discard in hearts.

Note that South had to avoid two traps. One was to cash the heart ace too early, after the heart finesse had won: in that case

West might have been able to ruff an early diamond lead and play the heart king, forcing South to rely on a club finesse.

The second trap was to leave the heart ace until too late. If South had led to the club ace after the first diamond ruff, he would have run the risk not only of a first-round club ruff but also of the actual distribution: West would have discarded his heart king on the fourth diamond lead, and made two tricks at the finish—a trump and the club king.

The reader who can follow this analysis deserves a word of commendation. And the rider who worked it out before getting to Grand Central deserves a free commuter ticket.

Making the Most of a
Single Suit

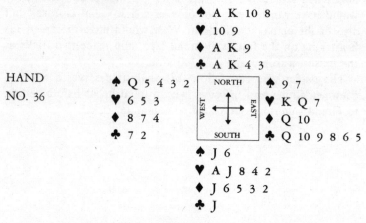

HAND
NO. 36

North and South vulnerable. The bidding:

South (D)	West	North	East
Pass	Pass	2 NT	Pass
3 ♣	Pass	3 ♠	Pass
4 ♦	Pass	5 ♦	Pass
6 ♦	Pass	Pass	Pass

West led the club seven

The right way to handle a single suit combination is generally considered elementary, but some such combinations have unexpected angles. Consider this:

NORTH

♦ A K 9

SOUTH

♦ J 6 5 3 2

The correct play depends on how many tricks South is trying to make from the suit. If four tricks are enough, there is a standard safety-play. South must cash the ace or king and use another suit to re-enter the closed hand. A low diamond is led, and the nine is played from dummy if West follows with a low card. This plan gives South four tricks unless all five missing diamonds are in one hand.

If the declarer needs five diamond tricks he must hope that the queen will fall under the ace-king: this is slightly better on a percentage basis than leading directly to the nine in the hope that West has Q 10 x.

A delicate point arises when the queen falls from the right-hand opponent on the first trick, and this was highlighted for this department by a remarkable coincidence. The right play of this combination was discussed by Oswald Jacoby of Dallas in an issue of The Bridge World, and by the same mail delivery we received a letter from Alfred Coane of Margate City, N.J., describing the diagrammed deal. It was played in the Mixed Pair event in the Asbury Park Regional Championships and Mr Coane and his wife gained a top score by bidding and making six diamonds.

South's bidding was optimistic even on the assumption that North's two no-trumps opening bid showed an old-fashioned 22-24 points rather than the modern 20-22. A simple response of three hearts would have permitted the partnership to rest safely in three no-trumps, but the actual Stayman bid of three clubs, asking for a major suit, led into deep water.

When South showed the diamond suit, concealing the hearts altogether, North had little choice but to raise. South then continued to slam on the theory that game in the minor suit was unlikely to produce a good score in a match-point event—other players were likely to reach game in no-trumps or hearts and achieve higher scores.

South won the club seven in the dummy with the king and played the diamond ace, dropping the ten from East. The only hope now was that the queen would fall, and it did.

It was then a simple matter to draw the remaining trump, cross to dummy with a spade lead, and attack hearts. This suit lay favourably, and the slam was made.

When the session was over, Mr and Mrs Coane discussed the deal with an anonymous stranger who had a sad story to tell. He had also reached six diamonds, and received the same lead.

But when he led the ace of trumps from dummy, East played the queen. This startling falsecard was both brilliant and correct, and it fooled South. He led a heart at the third trick, captured East's queen with the ace, and confidently finessed the diamond nine. East produced the ten, and the contract was down one.

South began to wonder whether he was playing against an expert he did not know by sight, but the young lady on his right looked innocent and inexperienced.

'That was a fine play you made in trumps,' he told her. The reply to this compliment was a surprise to him.

'Oh, I always play high-low with a doubleton.'

Getting Rid of an Unwanted King; or Let Them Eat Crow

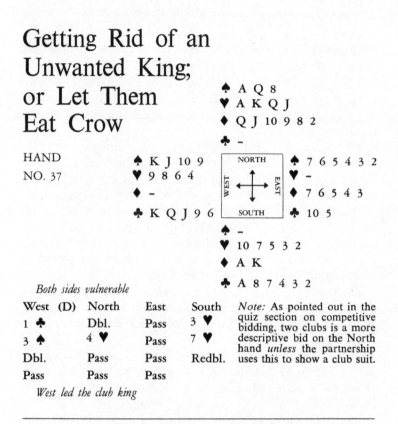

North (dummy):
♠ A Q 8
♥ A K Q J
♦ Q J 10 9 8 2
♣ -

West:
♠ K J 10 9
♥ 9 8 6 4
♦ -
♣ K Q J 9 6

East:
♠ 7 6 5 4 3 2
♥ -
♦ 7 6 5 4 3
♣ 10 5

South:
♠ -
♥ 10 7 5 3 2
♦ A K
♣ A 8 7 4 3 2

Both sides vulnerable

West (D)	North	East	South
1 ♣	Dbl.	Pass	3 ♥
3 ♠	4 ♥	Pass	7 ♥
Dbl.	Pass	Pass	Redbl.
Pass	Pass	Pass	

West led the club king

Note: As pointed out in the quiz section on competitive bidding, two clubs is a more descriptive bid on the North hand *unless* the partnership uses this to show a club suit.

Getting rid of a king who is blocking the road to liberty is a revolutionary proceeding which may be as necessary in bridge as it is in history. The diagrammed deal, forwarded by Captain Edgar Peixotto, living appropriately in the Boulevard du Roi, Versailles, France, proves the point.

As this deal has a very long history, going back before the days of contract bridge, a modest exercise of anachronistic imagination can set the scene in the French Court in 1789. North is the ill-fated Louis XVI, well-meaning but weak. South is Queen Marie Antoinette, beautiful but poorly educated and shockingly extravagant. West is a soldier who believes in showing his strength. And East is a courtier who knows that he should not intervene in a royal dialogue.

The science of bidding was in a primitive state in those far-off days, but this does not entirely explain the strange North-South bidding. We must do a little mind-reading.

The King: 'This is a great hand. I suppose I could show it by a cue bid of two clubs. But Marie might think I have a club suit, and I should hate to have to play two clubs. A take-out double seems my safest move.'

The Queen: 'I'm glad I've got Louis into a bridge game. Perhaps it'll take his mind off his troubles with the Estates General. This looks like a good hand and I suppose I had better bid hearts. I think he could pass two hearts, so I'll bid three hearts.'

The King: 'I wonder what she means by that. It should be pre-emptive, but I'm not sure she is up to that. If she has a good hand she might not think of making a cue bid of two clubs, but I don't see how she can be strong with the hand I've got when West has bid twice. I'll just bid four hearts.'

The Queen: 'I have a feeling that old pessimist over there has more than he has shown me. I have control of all the side-suits, and I like bidding slams. Let's surprise them. Seven hearts.'

The King: 'Mon Dieu!'

The Queen: 'The impertinence of that old marshal, doubling me! I expect he has the heart king and thinks it is a trick. Won't he be surprised to see the ace in the dummy? I redouble on principle.'

Louis laid down his cards and said, 'I think you'll like the dummy, my dear.'

The Queen: 'Oh, thank you, Louis. It's a lovely dummy and I'm going to make it easily. Let me see. I will have six trump tricks, six diamonds and two black aces. Nothing to it. I will discard a spade from dummy, win with the ace of clubs and draw trumps.'

But Marie had a surprise on the second trick when East played a spade on the first round of trumps. The easy slam was not so easy after all. Then she saw a ray of daylight.

'I'm not dead yet. I can ruff the queen of spades, cash the king of diamonds and draw trumps. Then I can discard the diamond ace on the spade ace—a beautiful play—and make the diamonds in dummy.'

She tried this plan, but West ruffed the king of diamonds.

The Queen: 'It's not fair! *He* didn't have any trumps, and now *you* haven't any diamonds. It was a beautiful slam, and it was ruined by that *silly* distribution. I hate bridge! I'm not going to play any more!'

She left the room in mounting hysteria, followed closely by the King. East and West discussed the deal.

'I wouldn't have dared to tell her,' remarked the courtier, a good bridge player as well as the soul of tact, 'but she should have made it.

'Let me show you, mon vieux. The idea is to get the closed hand with one fewer trump than the open. She should have discarded a diamond from dummy at the first trick, not a spade. Then she can win in her hand with the club ace, lead a trump to dummy and ruff a spade. Another trump lead and another spade ruff leaves the queen with one trump and dummy with two. Then she can draw trumps, discarding the ace of diamonds, and then get rid of the king of diamonds on the spade ace.

'It is sad for France that the royal family does not have any foresight. The Bourbons cannot conceive that it might be right to get rid of a king.'

A Case of 'Off-Track' Bidding?

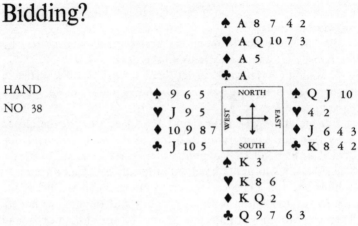

HAND
NO 38

	♠ A 8 7 4 2	
	♥ A Q 10 7 3	
	♦ A 5	
	♣ A	
♠ 9 6 5	NORTH	♠ Q J 10
♥ J 9 5	WEST ←→ EAST	♥ 4 2
♦ 10 9 8 7		♦ J 6 4 3
♣ J 10 5	SOUTH	♣ K 8 4 2
	♠ K 3	
	♥ K 8 6	
	♦ K Q 2	
	♣ Q 9 7 6 3	

North and South vulnerable

East (D)	South	West	North
Pass	Pass	3 ♦	4 ♦
5 ♦	6 NT	Pass	Pass
Dbl.	Redbl.	Pass	Pass
Pass			

West led the club jack

The tournament bridge world contains a number of eccentrics whose chief delight is to make weird bids and dislocate the normal bidding. There is one situation that invariably provokes their wildest excesses—not vulnerable against vulnerable, and in third seat with a weak hand.

One of these jokers was at work on the diagrammed deal played in a recent regional championship.

South opened the door for West when he decided to pass in second seat with a 13-point aceless hand that most experts, but not all, would open. It was now clear to West that his opponents held a game or slam, and that it was up to him to confuse the issue. So he bid three diamonds.

West's antics might perhaps have been successful if North had made a take-out double. East would have jumped to five diamonds, an advance save, and it would be difficult for North-South to reach their best contract, six hearts.

Instead North made a cue bid of four diamonds. East still thought it right to crowd the action with five diamonds. Now South had to guess what to do, and quite reasonably he guessed to bid six no-trumps. East doubled on rather questionable principles, and South redoubled with rather more reason.

There would have been no story if West had led a diamond, for South would simply have established spades. But West led the club jack, making the best move for the defence largely by accident.

South was Steve Sion of New York. He did not like his prospects. Other declarers would be in six hearts, having no trouble, and he was stuck in six no-trumps redoubled with only 11 tricks in view.

There was nothing for it but to lead out winners and pray for rain. So he won the first trick with the club ace and cashed five rounds of hearts. East had to make three discards, and gave up two diamonds, obviously useless in view of his partner's opening bid, and one club. West also discarded diamonds. The declarer next cashed the ace and king of diamonds, leaving himself on lead in this position:

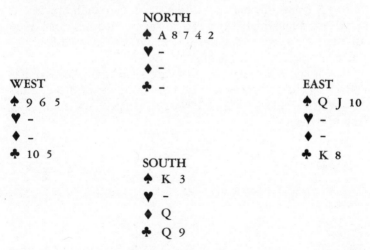

```
                    NORTH
                    ♠ A 8 7 4 2
                    ♥ -
                    ♦ -
WEST                ♣ -                    EAST
♠ 9 6 5                                    ♠ Q J 10
♥ -                                        ♥ -
♦ -                                        ♦ -
♣ 10 5                                     ♣ K 8
                    SOUTH
                    ♠ K 3
                    ♥ -
                    ♦ Q
                    ♣ Q 9
```

By the time South got over the shock of realising that East-West had begun with four diamonds each, he found that he knew the position. There were only black cards left, and it was highly probable that East and West had each retained three spades and two clubs. And the opening lead made it clear that East held the club king and West the ten.

The lead of the diamond queen ruined both defenders in turn. If West had discarded a club South would have played the queen at the next trick, pinning the ten and establishing the nine as the 12th trick. So West threw a spade, and left his partner with no recourse. Throwing a spade at this point would have given South an overtrick, so East gave up the eight of clubs. The declarer confidently led the club nine, and claimed the contract when the king appeared.

'You didn't have to double', grumbled West to his partner after a little work with a pocket calculator had established that the score was 2,060 to North-South. 'We would have had a top because they make a trick more in hearts.'

'I'm afraid I didn't know you had made one of your clever openings with a balanced yarborough,' retorted East. 'Even as it was, he had to play well to make it. There was no defence.'

'There certainly wasn't at the finish,' agreed South. 'But suppose you keep all your diamonds and give up a spade or two?'

Inspection showed that even this double-dummy plan would not have helped the defence. East's last discard on hearts would have forced him to give up a second spade, exposing West's nine to a finesse; a second club discard would have allowed South to force out the king and establish the queen.

East would have been able to defend successfully keeping diamonds only if his partner had held the spade eight instead of the six. Which finally proved that West's opening bid was not *quite* strong enough.

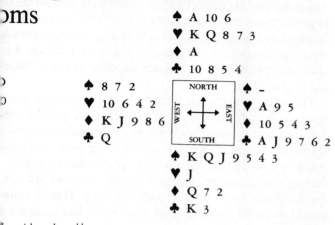

♠ A 10 6
♥ K Q 8 7 3
♦ A
♣ 10 8 5 4

♠ 8 7 2
♥ 10 6 4 2
♦ K J 9 8 6
♣ Q

♠ -
♥ A 9 5
♦ 10 5 4 3
♣ A J 9 7 6 2

♠ K Q J 9 5 4 3
♥ J
♦ Q 7 2
♣ K 3

er side vulnerable

(D)	East	South	West
	2 ♣	2 ♠	Pass
	Pass	4 NT	Pass
	Pass	5 ♠	Pass
	Pass		

led the club queen

good bridge player has a sixth sense telling him, even
hings look calmest, that disaster is impending. It is then,
is antennae begin to quiver in bidding or in play, that he
avoids the usual and the routine, and searches for the
and the spectacular.

idding, for example, suppose you hold the following:

♠ 4
♥ Q 6 5
♦ 10 7 6 4 3 2
♣ 6 5 3

Battles of Wits

Ruff Your Partner's Trick—
If its the Winning Defence

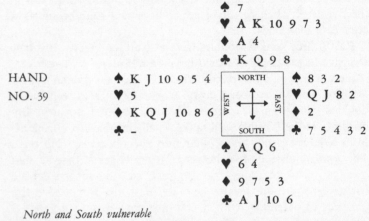

♠ 7
♥ A K 10 9 7 3
♦ A 4
♣ K Q 9 8

HAND
NO. 39

♠ K J 10 9 5 4
♥ 5
♦ K Q J 10 8 6
♣ -

♠ 8 3 2
♥ Q J 8 2
♦ 2
♣ 7 5 4 3 2

♠ A Q 6
♥ 6 4
♦ 9 7 5 3
♣ A J 10 6

North and South vulnerable

South (D)	West	North	East
Pass	1 ♠	Dbl.	Pass
2 NT	4 ♦	Dbl.	4 ♠
4 NT	Pass	5 ♥	Dbl.
Pass	Pass	5 NT	Dbl.
6 ♣	Pass	Pass	Dbl.
Pass	Pass	Pass	

Note: We do not recommend North's original take-out double, preferring the much more descriptive bid of three hearts (strong).

West led the diamond king

Trumping his partner's ace was the worst crime in the book for
the old-fashioned whist player. Bridge players know better: it is
often right for a defender to ruff a trick that his partner has
already won or looks as though he will win. Or, rather, they
usually know better, even though the diagrammed deal, played
in a New York rubber bridge game, shows a slip-up.

A curious feature of the sensational and complicated auction was that West, with a powerful freak hand, did much less bidding than the other players at the table. He opened with one spade, showed his distribution by jumping to four diamonds on the next round, and subsided thereafter.

North's take-out double of one spade was in order according to American methods, for his hand was much too strong for a simple overcall of two hearts. But his second double at the four level was clumsy, forcing him eventually to bid his heart suit at the five level when he might better have said four hearts right after four diamonds.

East's three penalty doubles were also all too greedy. It is true that five hearts doubled would have been beaten—by two tricks, if there had been an inspired club lead—and that five no-trumps doubled would have been down at least two tricks. But East's doubles, based on his partner's bidding and the apparent uncertainty in the North-South ranks, finally harried his opponents from a hopeless no-trump pillar into an unbeatable club post. The loud double of five hearts convinced North that he had made an error in trying that contract, and the second double frightened South into a safer six clubs. East was overjoyed at the prospect of defending with five trumps, but was underjoyed a few minutes later.

West led the diamond king and South decided quickly on his line of play. He won with the diamond ace in dummy, and returned the diamond four. East, knowing that his partner would be able to win the trick, happily discarded a spade without considering the possibility of a ruff.

That was the end of the defence. West won and led a third round of diamonds, hoping that his partner would be able to overruff. But he couldn't beat the dummy's eight, and after that trick South was able to cash his three tricks in the major suits and cross-ruff. He made in all eight trump tricks and four top tricks in the side suits. East's trump length was useless to him: He was underruffing helplessly on the last five tricks.

(Paradoxically, the slam would have failed against a 'better' trump division. If West had one trump instead of a void, he would have had two chances to make a killing trump lead or could have ruffed South's second heart winner.)

'I could have beaten it,' announced E
seen, too late, that he should have ruffe
diamonds rather than let his partner
trump. Ruffing his partner's trick would h
to seven trump tricks in all, and a total
South—Lee Hazen, a former world cham
serves as counsel for the American Co
made what seemed to be a generous off
like to play it again?'

The offer was happily accepted, an
structed. As before, South won the first
ace. East had a trump ready for the dia
Hazen did not oblige him: 'If you're go
going to play better,' he said. He mac
dummy's spade seven, won it with the
queen. When West covered with the k
carded dummy's diamond loser. East ne
the lead and play a trump.

Hazen would certainly have found th
'scissors coup'—in a tournament, for ca
when prestige is at stake. Playing for m
is expected, and the best plays—for bot
until the post-mortem stage.

Battles of Wits

Ruff Your Partner's Trick—
If its the Winning Defence

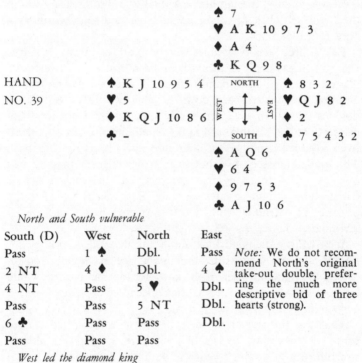

```
                                    ♠ 7
                                    ♥ A K 10 9 7 3
                                    ♦ A 4
                                    ♣ K Q 9 8
HAND           ♠ K J 10 9 5 4    NORTH      ♠ 8 3 2
NO. 39         ♥ 5                           ♥ Q J 8 2
               ♦ K Q J 10 8 6    WEST  EAST  ♦ 2
               ♣ -                SOUTH      ♣ 7 5 4 3 2
                                    ♠ A Q 6
                                    ♥ 6 4
                                    ♦ 9 7 5 3
                                    ♣ A J 10 6
```

North and South vulnerable

South (D)	West	North	East	
Pass	1 ♠	Dbl.	Pass	*Note:* We do not recom-
2 NT	4 ♦	Dbl.	4 ♠	mend North's original take-out double, prefer-
4 NT	Pass	5 ♥	Dbl.	ring the much more descriptive bid of three
Pass	Pass	5 NT	Dbl.	hearts (strong).
6 ♣	Pass	Pass	Dbl.	
Pass	Pass	Pass		

West led the diamond king

Trumping his partner's ace was the worst crime in the book for the old-fashioned whist player. Bridge players know better: it is often right for a defender to ruff a trick that his partner has already won or looks as though he will win. Or, rather, they *usually* know better, even though the diagrammed deal, played in a New York rubber bridge game, shows a slip-up.

A curious feature of the sensational and complicated auction was that West, with a powerful freak hand, did much less bidding than the other players at the table. He opened with one spade, showed his distribution by jumping to four diamonds on the next round, and subsided thereafter.

North's take-out double of one spade was in order according to American methods, for his hand was much too strong for a simple overcall of two hearts. But his second double at the four level was clumsy, forcing him eventually to bid his heart suit at the five level when he might better have said four hearts right after four diamonds.

East's three penalty doubles were also all too greedy. It is true that five hearts doubled would have been beaten—by two tricks, if there had been an inspired club lead—and that five no-trumps doubled would have been down at least two tricks. But East's doubles, based on his partner's bidding and the apparent uncertainty in the North-South ranks, finally harried his opponents from a hopeless no-trump pillar into an unbeatable club post. The loud double of five hearts convinced North that he had made an error in trying that contract, and the second double frightened South into a safer six clubs. East was overjoyed at the prospect of defending with five trumps, but was underjoyed a few minutes later.

West led the diamond king and South decided quickly on his line of play. He won with the diamond ace in dummy, and returned the diamond four. East, knowing that his partner would be able to win the trick, happily discarded a spade without considering the possibility of a ruff.

That was the end of the defence. West won and led a third round of diamonds, hoping that his partner would be able to overruff. But he couldn't beat the dummy's eight, and after that trick South was able to cash his three tricks in the major suits and cross-ruff. He made in all eight trump tricks and four top tricks in the side suits. East's trump length was useless to him: He was underruffing helplessly on the last five tricks.

(Paradoxically, the slam would have failed against a 'better' trump division. If West had one trump instead of a void, he would have had two chances to make a killing trump lead or could have ruffed South's second heart winner.)

'I could have beaten it,' announced East dejectedly. He had seen, too late, that he should have ruffed the second round of diamonds rather than let his partner take it and then led a trump. Ruffing his partner's trick would have limited the declarer to seven trump tricks in all, and a total of 11 tricks. Thereupon South—Lee Hazen, a former world championship contender who serves as counsel for the American Contract Bridge League—made what seemed to be a generous offer to East: 'Would you like to play it again?'

The offer was happily accepted, and the hand was reconstructed. As before, South won the first trick with the diamond ace. East had a trump ready for the diamond continuation, but Hazen did not oblige him: 'If you're going to defend better, I'm going to play better,' he said. He made the sure play of the dummy's spade seven, won it with the ace and led the spade queen. When West covered with the king, Hazen simply discarded dummy's diamond loser. East never had a chance to gain the lead and play a trump.

Hazen would certainly have found this latter manoeuvre—the 'scissors coup'—in a tournament, for careful thought is normal when prestige is at stake. Playing for mere money a rapid tempo is expected, and the best plays—for both sides—may lie hidden until the post-mortem stage.

The Sixth Sense: Knowing When Disaster Looms

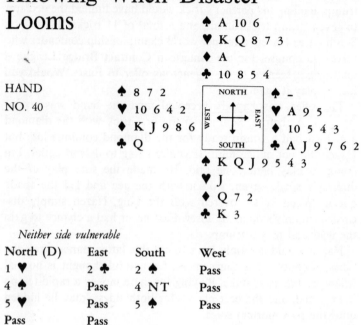

♠ A 10 6
♥ K Q 8 7 3
♦ A
♣ 10 8 5 4

HAND NO. 40

♠ 8 7 2
♥ 10 6 4 2
♦ K J 9 8 6
♣ Q

NORTH
WEST — EAST
SOUTH

♠ —
♥ A 9 5
♦ 10 5 4 3
♣ A J 9 7 6 2

♠ K Q J 9 5 4 3
♥ J
♦ Q 7 2
♣ K 3

Neither side vulnerable

North (D)	East	South	West
1 ♥	2 ♣	2 ♠	Pass
4 ♠	Pass	4 NT	Pass
5 ♥	Pass	5 ♠	Pass
Pass	Pass		

West led the club queen

Every good bridge player has a sixth sense telling him, even when things look calmest, that disaster is impending. It is then, when his antennae begin to quiver in bidding or in play, that he pauses, avoids the usual and the routine, and searches for the bizarre and the spectacular.

In bidding, for example, suppose you hold the following:

♠ 4
♥ Q 6 5
♦ 10 7 6 4 3 2
♣ 6 5 3

You are vulnerable against non-vulnerable opponents. Your left-hand opponent deals and bids one diamond, your partner makes a take-out double, and the player on your right redoubles.

Now the standard procedure when you have no available suit is to pass and let your partner find his own way out of the mess, but that would be a short-sighted policy here. Left to himself, your partner will most likely bid one spade. The opponents will double and you are likely to go down 500 points; any further wriggling and you may get hit for 800 or even 1100 in penalties.

One heart, however—the bid you would have made if there had been a pass on your right—would be far better. It is a practical contract, and even if it is doubled it might not go down at all if the opponents fail to lead trumps quickly. It's an unusual and even risky bid, but one inspired by a sixth sense.

In the play of the hand, too, there may be a case for unusual action if the sixth-sense antennae are alert. The diagrammed deal, played in a Nassau-Suffolk Knockout Championship, gave Merle Tom of New York, sitting South, a chance to make a brilliant deceptive play.

North's opening bid of one heart, East's overcall of two clubs, and South's bid of two spades were obvious actions. North should then have been content to raise to three spades, and his jump to game caused South to visualise a slam. He used Blackwood to ask for aces, but had to sign off in five spades when his partner indicated only two aces. He felt confident of making 11 tricks.

But when West led the club queen and the dummy came down with four in that suit, South had to revise his opinion. His antennae told him he was in trouble with the clubs.

An overcall at the two level normally indicates a six-card suit or a strong five-card suit, and South knew that it was most unlikely that East overcalled two clubs with a suit no better than A J 9 x x. He inferred a six-card suit, a singleton queen lead—and disaster. It was clear that the defenders were about to make the club ace, a club ruff and the heart ace. Down one. North-South were headed for the most humiliating result in bridge: being set in five of a major reached voluntarily.

So South had to find a brilliant stroke to lead the defence astray. When East won the first trick with the club ace, South dropped his king without hesitation, thus convincing East that the missing three was in the West hand.

East could see no future in playing a second club, and had to search for a possible third trick for the defence. There was just a chance from his angle that his partner held three trumps headed by the queen. If so, by forcing dummy to ruff, East could keep the declarer from cashing the spade king and thus from finessing against the queen on the second round of trumps. With that in mind he returned a diamond, clearing dummy's singleton ace.

South then led the heart three from dummy, giving East a chance to slip and play low, but he put up the ace. East had a last chance to cash the club jack, but he was still under the spell of South's brilliant deception at the first trick. He led a second diamond, and the play was over. South ruffed in dummy, discarded his club loser on the heart king, and could either ruff or discard his diamond queen.

This deal illustrates the importance of stopping to think the hand through when the dummy first appears. If declarer stopped to think *after* East had played the club ace the situation would be clear to the defence. The sixth sense needs a little help, after all, from the common.

How to Become an Insomniac

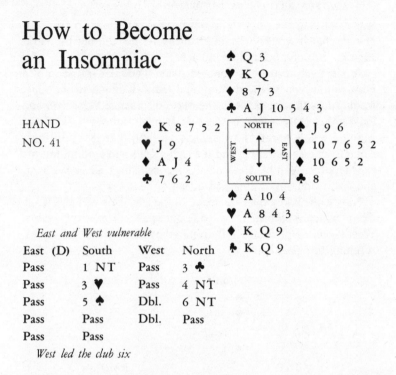

                    ♠ Q 3
                    ♥ K Q
                    ♦ 8 7 3
                    ♣ A J 10 5 4 3

HAND   ♠ K 8 7 5 2   NORTH   ♠ J 9 6
NO. 41   ♥ J 9   ♥ 10 7 6 5 2
            ♦ A J 4   WEST   EAST   ♦ 10 6 5 2
            ♣ 7 6 2   SOUTH   ♣ 8

                    ♠ A 10 4
                    ♥ A 8 4 3
                    ♦ K Q 9
                    ♣ K Q 9

East and West vulnerable

East (D)	South	West	North
Pass	1 NT	Pass	3 ♣
Pass	3 ♥	Pass	4 NT
Pass	5 ♠	Dbl.	6 NT
Pass	Pass	Dbl.	Pass
Pass	Pass		

West led the club six

Bridge is not a game for those with a tendency to insomnia, a complaint which may afflict even international players when they have failed to measure up to their own standards. The diagrammed deal from the 1969's world championship resulted in a sleepless Brazilian.

The opening bid of one no-trump showed 17-20 points in the Roman System, and the jump response of three clubs asked South to show the strength of his hand and the quality of his clubs. His bid of three hearts showed good club support but a minimum hand, which was good enough to induce North to launch into a variation of Blackwood. The response of five spades showed two aces of the same rank—both major or both minor.

West's double of five spades and his subsequent double of North's six no-trumps bid were misguided. The possible profit was small and the possible loss was substantial—apart from the chance that it would help South to make his contract by marking the position of the diamond ace.

Against six no-trumps doubled, West made the safe lead of a club. South won in the dummy and led a diamond to the king, leading to a crucial point in the play. In practice West won and led another club, a play not as safe as might appear.

South could count 11 tricks, and realised that the 12th must come from a squeeze. He had the right idea up to a point, but his execution was faulty. He took the second club lead in his hand and cashed dummy's king and queen of hearts.

Next came a key play—a spade to the ace. This was a 'Vienna Coup' which established the spade queen as a threat card against West's king. But South fell from grace—he cashed his clubs, reaching this position:

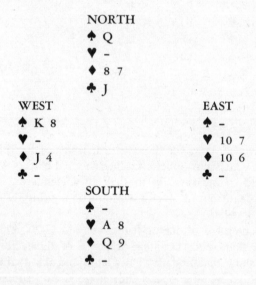

```
                    NORTH
                    ♠ Q
                    ♥ -
                    ♦ 8 7
                    ♣ J
    WEST                        EAST
    ♠ K 8                       ♠ -
    ♥ -                         ♥ 10 7
    ♦ J 4                       ♦ 10 6
    ♣ -                         ♣ -
                    SOUTH
                    ♠ -
                    ♥ A 8
                    ♦ Q 9
                    ♣ -
```

The last club from dummy forced East to throw the diamond six, but West was in no trouble. He could part with the spade eight and South had to lose another trick.

South should have cashed the heart ace after the spade ace. In the end-position, compared with the one shown, West would have had a spade less, North a diamond less and East a heart less. The play of the last club would then have executed a true double squeeze. East would have to keep his heart winner and West his spade winner, so South's diamond nine would win the last trick.

South was upset by his error, which was enough to keep anyone awake at night. And from that point on the Brazilians never reached the peak form in which they had begun the tournament.

If the contract had been made, Brazil would have gained 12 international match points instead of losing 11.

South's double squeeze could have been broken up by the attacking return of a diamond, either the jack or the four, after the diamond ace wins the second trick. This drives out the entry South needs to his hand in the end-position.

Such a defence is not impossible, for all the high honours are marked in the South hand by the bidding. West must assume that his partner has the diamond ten, for otherwise there is no hope for the defence against accurate play by the declarer.

West would also have had to reproach himself for doubling. If he had stayed silent, he could have afforded to duck the first diamond lead and wait for South to lead the suit again—the declarer would not then have known that an endplay was possible in spades and diamonds.

As it was, West was lucky that he was not the victim of insomnia.

A Worthless Card May
Have a Commercial Value
for the Defence

```
                                    ♠ 6 4
                                    ♥ A K 7 3
                                    ♦ A 10 6
                                    ♣ A Q 7 2
HAND              ♠ K 9 8 3   NORTH        ♠ J 10 5
NO. 42            ♥ J 10 9 8              ♥ 6 4
                  ♦ K 9 3   WEST    EAST   ♦ 8 7 4 2
                  ♣ 10 6     SOUTH         ♣ 9 8 4 3
                                    ♠ A Q 7 2
                                    ♥ Q 5 2
                                    ♦ Q J 5
                                    ♣ K J 5
```

Both sides vulnerable

South (D)	West	North	East
1 NT	Pass	6 NT	Pass
Pass	Pass		

West led the heart jack

Players who find themselves defending with a completely useless hand, lacking any trick-taking possibility, can be forgiven for assuming that they can play cards at random without affecting the issue. But on occasions a worthless card may be of vital importance. If East had discarded the 13th diamond in the diagrammed deal, an apparently useless card for which there was no conceivable entry, the declarer would have had no trouble making the slam.

The bidding was rough and ready, but there was nothing wrong with the final contract. South's opening bid of one no-trump was one point short of the normal 16-18 standard, but many partnerships accept a 15-point minimum.

As it happened, West had an obvious safe lead, the heart jack. South counted 10 sure tricks: four clubs, three hearts, two diamonds and one spade. Spades, hearts and diamonds each offered a chance of an extra trick, and South needed two of them to

work. This represents a slightly inferior slam, but as the play
showed there was also an endplay possibility.

South won the first trick with the heart queen and led the
diamond queen. West covered with the king and the prospects of
success increased considerably. The declarer won with the ace in
dummy and cashed all his winners except the major-suit aces. He
took four club tricks, two more diamond tricks and the heart
king—nine down, three to go—to reach this position:

```
                      NORTH
                      ♠ 6 4
                      ♥ A 7
      WEST            ♦ -            EAST
      ♠ K 9           ♣ -            ♠ J 10 5
      ♥ 10 9                        ♥ -
      ♦ -                           ♦ 8
      ♣ -                           ♣ -
                      SOUTH
                      ♠ A Q 7
                      ♥ 5
                      ♦ -
                      ♣ -
```

South could see three chances of landing the slam: the heart
suit might break, making his seven a winner; the spade finesse
might work; or a lead of the fourth round of hearts might endplay West and force him to lead into the ace-queen of spades at
the 12th trick.

This throw-in play would have worked as the cards lie, and
would have been an automatic proposition but for one thing: the
13th diamond. South was afraid of giving up a heart to West in
case he also had that good diamond, which would be the setting
trick.

While South was thinking, East—Barbara Daglian of Dobbs
Ferry, New York—had been thinking also. South had produced
nine high-card points in hearts, diamonds and clubs. That meant
he had at least six points in spades to make up his 15-point
minimum. Now, if South had ace-king of spades of course he
had 12 top tricks and there was no hope for the defence. So East

decided that the only hope was to assume the ace-queen of spades in the South hand, counting on her partner to have the king.

But she didn't stop there. She realised that the king might not be good for a trick if South decided on the endplay. How to keep South from the throw-in? Obviously by leading him to think that the good 13th diamond was in *West's* hand.

So when South led the heart ace from the dummy, East was ready. She quickly made the fine play of discarding a spade, in spite of the fact that the spade holding represented a potential trick and the diamond eight did not.

South fell into the trap. Unsure about the location of the diamond, he was inclined to think that West had it—East would have had no reason, apparently, to keep a useless winner. South finally decided to avoid the endplay and finesse the spade queen, and West made two tricks to defeat the contract—thanks to East's presence of mind in retaining her 'worthless' diamond.

The last diamond, interestingly enough, would have been equally important if West had held that card together with the spade king and the heart stopper. If he had discarded the diamond in order to keep guards in both spades and hearts, South would have had the same guaranteed endplay by leading the fourth round of hearts. The only defence would be for West to unguard his spade king. If he did this without any revealing hesitation South would almost certainly misjudge the situation.

Look for the Lurking Danger—then Find a Clever Counter

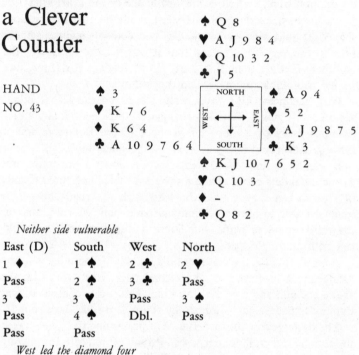

♠ Q 8
♥ A J 9 8 4
♦ Q 10 3 2
♣ J 5

HAND
NO. 43

♠ 3
♥ K 7 6
♦ K 6 4
♣ A 10 9 7 6 4

NORTH
WEST · EAST
SOUTH

♠ A 9 4
♥ 5 2
♦ A J 9 8 7 5
♣ K 3

♠ K J 10 7 6 5 2
♥ Q 10 3
♦ -
♣ Q 8 2

Neither side vulnerable

East (D)	South	West	North
1 ♦	1 ♠	2 ♣	2 ♥
Pass	2 ♠	3 ♣	Pass
3 ♦	3 ♥	Pass	3 ♠
Pass	4 ♠	Dbl.	Pass
Pass	Pass		

West led the diamond four

A declarer who makes an assumption may be clever or foolish according to circumstances. A famous French expert found himself in both categories on the deal shown in the diagram. The contract is four spades, and on the opening lead of the diamond four East plays the ace and South ruffs. What should South do next?

First he should judge from the bidding the high-card strength of each opponent. East opened one diamond, but was passive thereafter except for a belated diamond rebid; he is likely to have 12 high-card points. West has bid and rebid clubs, and has doubled four spades, suggesting about 10 points. His failure to lead clubs indicates that he does not have both ace and king of his own suit and it is, therefore, likely that he has two other honours—probably the diamond king, since East played the ace on the first trick, and either the spade ace or the heart king.

On the basis of this analysis South made his first assumption: that West holds the heart king. The decision was made easier for him by the very good reason that it was the only hope for the contract. If East held that card the defenders had four sure tricks: two clubs, one heart and the trump ace.

With the heart king favourably placed on the left it might seem easy to make 10 tricks: six spades, three hearts, and either a fourth heart or a club ruff in the dummy. But there was a lurking danger and South spotted it—the spade nine.

It was likely that West held six clubs and East a doubleton, so the defenders could create a problem by leading three rounds of clubs when they gained the lead with the spade ace. East might be able to overruff dummy's spade eight with the nine on the third round of clubs, but South would survive if he could ruff with dummy's spade queen.

As the cards lie, the contract fails quickly if South leads to the spade queen in dummy at the second trick. East wins with the spade ace and shifts to the club king. The suit is continued, and dummy's spade eight is topped by the nine on the third round.

The declarer saw the importance of preserving the spade queen in dummy for ruffing purposes. Proud of himself for having diagnosed the danger, South made his second assumption, this time a bad one: he assumed that East would take the trump ace immediately. At the second trick he led the spade ten.

A second after the card hit the table he cursed himself, for he had seen the flaw. East saw it also: he allowed the spade ten to win, and remained in control of the situation. South could do no better than lead a second round of trumps, and when East won he switched to the club king and continued the suit. When West won with the ace he played a third round and the spade nine was the setting trick.

What South should have done was to lead a club at the second trick, cutting the defenders' communications. He had to make sure that West would win his club trick while the spade queen was still available in the dummy for ruffing purposes.

If South follows this plan and leads a club, East wins with the king and is stuck. If he plays a second club and West wins and plays a third round, the declarer ruffs with dummy's spade queen. If East cashes the spade ace before leading the second round of clubs the result is the same. And if he plays the ace and another spade he removes the queen from the dummy but allows South to make an overtrick (East's remaining trump is drawn, and dummy's hearts provide discards for declarer's two remaining clubs).

East's best chance is to return a low trump at the third trick after winning with the club king. This forces South to continue with the communication-cutting plan by leading a second round of clubs.

If South had found the winning play at the table, a quick-thinking East would have had the chance to indulge in some unfair criticism. 'If you'd led a heart,' he could have told his partner, 'or even your trump, which I would have ducked, my spade nine would have given us the setting trick in all situations.'

The Urge to Protect His High Cards Led This Defender Astray

HAND NO. 44

```
                    ♠ J 9 4
                    ♥ A 6 3
                    ♦ 9 6 2
                    ♣ A Q 10 9
  ♠ Q 7 6 5 3    NORTH       ♠ K 10
  ♥ Q 9 7     WEST    EAST   ♥ K 8 5 4
  ♦ A 8 5                    ♦ 7 4
  ♣ K 3          SOUTH       ♣ J 8 7 5 2
                    ♠ A 8 2
                    ♥ J 10 2
                    ♦ K Q J 10 3
                    ♣ 6 4
```

Both sides vulnerable

South (D)	West	North	East
1 ♦	Pass	2 ♣	Pass
2 NT	Pass	3 NT	Pass
Pass	Pass		

West led the spade five

Note: Playing 'Utility' or Acol, South could not possibly rebid 2 NT so this is a game contract which might be missed—and rightly so!

The usual business of high cards is to capture inferior honours in the hand to the right. Thus, if the opening leader's partner has the king of the suit led, and if dummy has the queen or jack and plays low, he should normally play an intermediate card. For example:

♦ Q 6 4

West   East
♦ 5 led   ♦ K 10 7

In a no-trump contract the declarer plays dummy's six on the lead of the diamond five. East should play the ten, preserving the king to capture the queen later. This gains whenever South has the diamond ace.

The defender's problem is much more difficult if he has a doubleton king-ten. The play of the ten may still be right—if East is worried simply about saving a single trick. But if he is hoping to defeat the contract, he must make the right guess about the location of the jack. If his partner has it, with or without the ace, the ten is the right play; but if South has the jack, the play of the ten can be fatal. For if South started with J x x, and is allowed to take the trick with the jack, the suit will be blocked for the defence. When the defenders gain the lead, East's king can win the second diamond trick; but unless East has some other-than-diamond way to get to his partner's hand, West will be unable to take his ace and continue the suit.

A most unusual example of this point was described by Ernst Theimer of Rumson, N.J., in a magazine article. As the diagram shows, the bidding was highly optimistic. The deal might easily have been passed out, but South chose to open, impressed by the solidity of his diamond suit. North had enough to respond two clubs and to raise two no-trumps to game. Whether or not a two no-trumps rebid shows more than a minimum opening bid is a matter of partnership style. In this case, personalities intruded—South chose the bid because he distrusted his partner's playing ability and wanted to become the declarer.

A combined holding of 22 points rarely offers a sound play for game, and South's prospects in three no-trumps were not bright. He could see only seven seemingly sure tricks—four in diamonds and the three aces. And even the diamond tricks became uncertain with the opening lead. For if the opponents held up their diamond ace until the third round of the suit, the spade ace would be his only entry to his hand—and the lead of the spade five put that entry under immediate fire.

When dummy played low on the spade five, East put on the ten, the normal play. South ducked, and ducked again when the spade king was continued.

Had East then made a passive return, such as a diamond, South would have had little trouble. He would have driven out the diamond ace while the spade ace remained as an entry to his hand; eventually he would have made three club tricks and a heart or two clubs and two hearts, depending on the defence.

But East, after his spade king was allowed to hold, rose to the occasion by switching to the heart king. If South had fallen into the trap of winning in dummy, he would have been defeated. West would have been left with two entries, and would have established and cashed his spades before declarer could make nine tricks.

South, however, judged the position accurately and allowed East to win his second king. The diamond seven was the next lead, and West held up his diamond ace until the third round of the suit. He led a third round of spades, and South took the ace and his two remaining diamond winners.

South's last four cards were the J-10 of hearts and his two clubs, and he needed to win finesses in both suits. He led the heart jack, and it did not matter whether West covered or not— South could make the contract.

The winning defence, as South pointed out when the hand was over, was for East to play the spade king, not the ten, on the first trick. South can make two spade tricks by winning, but he thereby loses his entry for the diamonds. He does even worse by ducking, for East continues the ten, and West's spades are established before South's diamonds.

As it turned out, East's unwillingness to play an 'unnecessarily' high card on the opening trick was penny wise but pound foolish. He saved a trick here and lost a game there.

Even Experts May Grieve, When They Practice to Deceive

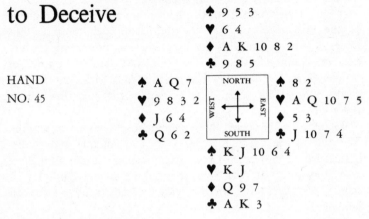

HAND NO. 45

North: ♠ 9 5 3 ♥ 6 4 ♦ A K 10 8 2 ♣ 9 8 5

West: ♠ A Q 7 ♥ 9 8 3 2 ♦ J 6 4 ♣ Q 6 2

East: ♠ 8 2 ♥ A Q 10 7 5 ♦ 5 3 ♣ J 10 7 4

South: ♠ K J 10 6 4 ♥ K J ♦ Q 9 7 ♣ A K 3

East and West vulnerable

South (D)	West	North	East
1 NT	Pass	2 NT	Pass
3 NT	Pass	Pass	Pass

West led the heart two

Rules of thumb have some value for the beginner, but they have to be hedged with 'if's and 'but's for the more experienced player. 'Third hand high' is a rule for beginners. 'Third hand high when dummy's holding is weak' is the version for intermediate players. And even that modified rule has an expert exception.

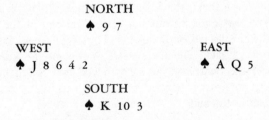

NORTH
♠ 9 7

WEST
♠ J 8 6 4 2

EAST
♠ A Q 5

SOUTH
♠ K 10 3

West leads the spade four in a no-trump contract, and the routine play for East is the ace. He continues with the queen, and South can hold up his king, shutting out West's long spades if East has an entry and West does not.

If East is an expert, however, he is more apt to play the queen on the first trick, breaking the third-hand-high rule; he thus forces South to win with the king, thereby preserving the defenders' communication in the suit. (At double-dummy, of course, South would play low on the first trick, but he can hardly afford that when West's lead might have been from A J x x x.)

But as often happens, the exception itself has an exception. The play of the queen is unnecessary and actually undesirable if East has no prospect of regaining the lead—it may fool West as well as South. If West gains the lead, he may give up playing spades, fearing to give South a trick by leading into an ace-ten holding.

A slight variation of this exception to the exception occurred on the diagrammed deal from the Spingold Knockout Team Championship final in Minneapolis in 1968. It was also an example of one of the ironies of the game, for the winners of the title reached an inferior contract and made it while their opponents reached a superior contract which failed.

The inferior contract was reached after Sam Kehela of Toronto, one of the world's greatest players, chose to open the South hand with one no-trump. He quickly regretted his bid when West led the heart two against three no-trumps and the dummy appeared. He could count eight tricks with a normal diamond distribution, but it was clear that before he could make his ninth trick in spades the defenders would get at least five tricks. It also seemed that four spades would have been a better contract.

Luckily for Kehela, the East player made a play on the first trick which was cunning but not clever. Instead of the normal play of the ace, he put on the queen. Thus West knew that South held the heart jack. He also knew, or thought he knew, that South held the heart ace. So he believed that South held two more heart stoppers when, in fact, East was sitting with four more tricks in the suit.

South, too, was deceived about the position of the heart ace. It was pointless to take eight tricks, for he would have no chance of a ninth that way, so he led to the diamond king in dummy and finessed the spade jack. He hoped that this would force the ace, and that West would then fail to continue hearts. For if West held the heart ace, as appeared to be the case, he would be reluctant to continue the suit, fearing to establish the jack in the South hand.

West *was* reluctant to continue hearts, but not for the reason South supposed. It seemed to West that South was thoroughly guarded in hearts, a misapprehension resulting from East's play of the queen at the first trick, so West looked elsewhere for tricks and led the club two.

South took East's club ten with his ace and led the spade four from his hand, giving West the last chance for the defence. If he had put up his spade ace and led a heart, the defenders would have had six tricks; but he was still under the spell of his partner's play to the first trick. He played low on the spade, the nine won in dummy and South ran for home with nine tricks—five diamonds, two clubs, one spade and one heart.

When the hand was replayed, South opened the bidding with one spade and eventually reached game in spades after North had supported the suit. Four spades was a perfectly good contract which would have made if East had held the spade queen. As it was, West led the club two, and the defenders made two spade tricks, a club and a heart.

A Falsecarder Can Spin a Tangled Web

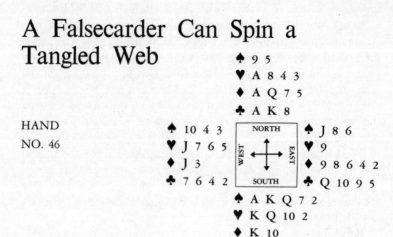

HAND

NO. 46

Neither side vulnerable

East (D)	South	West	North
Pass	1 ♠	Pass	3 ♦
Pass	3 ♥	Pass	4 ♥
Pass	4 NT	Pass	5 ♠
Pass	7 ♥	Pass	Pass
Pass			

West led the diamond jack

One of the most satisfying moments in bridge occurs when an alert defender is able to lead the declarer astray, causing him to abandon a winning path in favour of a losing one. One might say that deception arouses reflection and leads to deflection. Consider the following suit position:

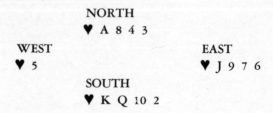

In an average game South has no difficulty. He cashes the heart king and leads to the ace in dummy. When West shows out on the second round, there is a marked finesse against East's jack. But if the players are expert, matters are more complicated.

When South leads the king of hearts, East drops the nine without any hesitation. If the nine is an honest card—that is, the lowest East has in the suit—it must be a singleton or part of a doubleton jack-nine holding. Any play by South will succeed if the suit breaks three-two, so South may assume a singleton nine. On that basis he will continue with the heart queen, expecting to trap the guarded jack in the West hand. However, West shows out and a trick has to be lost to the cunning East.

If South is expert and knows that East is capable of false-carding with the heart nine, he may see through the plot. East is three times as likely to have J 9 x x in the suit as he is to have a singleton nine, so the best play seems to be to lead to the ace after all, giving East credit for having falsecarded.

But there is slightly more to it than that, as shown by the diagrammed deal from the 1968 International Team Trials in Atlantic City, N.J. The fate of the seven-heart contract, as it turned out, depended on the opening lead. Paradoxically, the declarers who were presented with a trick by the lead went down, while the players who were giving nothing succeeded.

The lead of the diamond jack gave South four tricks in diamonds instead of three, but the gift was not significant. It was the play of the trump suit that mattered. After winning with the diamond king, South led the heart king and looked suspiciously at East's nine. He decided that this was more likely than not a falsecard, and he played to the heart ace in dummy at the third trick. West then had a sure trump trick, and the contract was defeated.

At the two tables at which the grand slam succeeded, the opening lead was a club, won in dummy with the king. A low heart was led, taken by the king in the closed hand. Again South looked suspiciously at the nine, but this time he had a different consideration to guide him.

The falsecard of the nine from J 9 x x is entirely safe for East if the king of hearts is led from the closed hand, but is apparently risky if a low card is led from the dummy. East would have to be afraid that such a falsecard might give South the contract if West happened to hold a singleton ten.

Suppose East held exactly J 9 6 5. In that case, the play of the nine could be fatal if West held the singleton ten. But if East has four trumps headed by the jack-nine-seven, he can afford the falsecard of the nine: his jack-seven will yield a trick if West has the ten.

As the falsecard is harder for East when the trumps are led from dummy, both declarers treated the nine as an honest play. They continued with the queen of hearts after the king and un-covered the trump situation. Drawing the missing trumps imme-diately with a finesse against West would have forced South to depend on a three-three spade break. Instead, he reverted to clubs, ruffing the third round with the ten in his own hand. The heart eight was finessed, the last trump was drawn, and the grand slam was a lay-down. South made five trump tricks, three spades, three diamonds and two clubs.

In the post-mortem, the players decided that after the diamond lead South should enter dummy with a club to play the first trump from dummy and so discourage the falsecard. But a brilliant East might figure out exactly why South took the trouble to enter dummy. Experts can produce a mighty com-plexity of deception and counterdeception from a single suit combination.

The Fine Art of Falsecarding—and How to Spot It

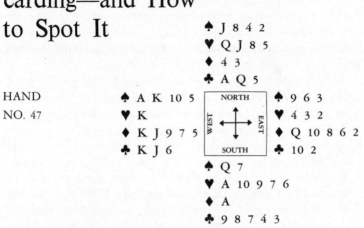

		♠ J 8 4 2	
		♥ Q J 8 5	
		♦ 4 3	
		♣ A Q 5	

HAND NO. 47

West			East
♠ A K 10 5			♠ 9 6 3
♥ K			♥ 4 3 2
♦ K J 9 7 5			♦ Q 10 8 6 2
♣ K J 6			♣ 10 2

	South	
	♠ Q 7	
	♥ A 10 9 7 6	
	♦ A	
	♣ 9 8 7 4 3	

East and West vulnerable

West (D)	North	East	South
1 ♦	Pass	Pass	1 ♥
Dbl.	Redbl.	2 ♦	3 ♣
Pass	4 ♥	Pass	Pass
Pass			

West led the spade king

Falsecarding is one of the most difficult defensive arts. Most inexperienced players fall into one of two categories: either they never falsecard at all, or they indulge in excessive random falsecards that deceive their partner more often than the declarer. It takes an expert defender to know the right moment to break the normal rules of defensive play—and an expert declarer to catch him at it.

On the diagrammed deal, a slightly modified version of a hand played in a top-level match, expert falsecarding led South and West into an entertaining battle of wits.

In the bidding, East passed his partner's opening one diamond, thus confessing extreme weakness. South made a protective bid of one heart, knowing that his partner must have a better hand than East, and probably much better. West's double was for take-out, as it almost always is at a low level when the doubler's partner has not bid; the fact that West himself has bid on the previous round does not affect the issue.

North's redouble showed general strength, not necessarily in hearts, just as if South's one heart had been an opening bid. East naturally showed his diamond support, and South ventured to bid his clubs at the level of three. North's jump to four hearts at this point was aggressive but not excessively so: he knew that his honour cards in hearts and clubs would fit his partner's hand.

If South's clubs had been slightly stronger, say J 10 x x x, the contract would have been an excellent one. Even as it was he had fair prospects. It was highly probable that West held the club king and that he could limit his losers outside the trump suit to three. The problem was to decide where the trump king was, and the play and reasoning can follow four different courses according to the standard of the players.

At the lowest level South will simply finesse trumps through his hand and hope that East has the king. This is the normal percentage play in default of other clues, for East is far more likely to have the king guarded than West to have it unguarded. As the cards lie, this play fails.

On a slightly higher level South can make some inferences from East's bidding and play. If West leads the spade king and then switches to a low diamond, East's queen is taken by the ace and South begins thinking. He can reason that East is most unlikely to have the heart king as well as the diamond queen, since good players rarely pass a minor-suit opening bid holding five points in high cards. West's bidding has also suggested a singleton heart, so the chance that it is the king is well worth taking. South should, therefore, judge that his best chance is to play the ace of hearts and hope to drop a singleton king in the West hand. This play works.

On the third level an expert West will appreciate the need to deprive South of the knowledge that East has the diamond queen. He will, therefore, lead the unsupported diamond *king*—

not a low diamond—at the second trick, a falsecard play to suggest to South that it comes from a king-queen combination and, therefore, that East does *not* have the queen of diamonds. This should convince South that East's points must lie in hearts, not diamonds and, therefore, that he might have the king of hearts. South will then have no reason to reject the normal heart finesse against East. Result: down one.

A former world champion who held the West cards made this fine falsecard of the diamond king. He was unlucky that the declarer was another former world champion who was able to play on the fourth level.

South knew that West was quite capable of falsecarding, and he carried the reasoning a stage further. Suppose West did hold the king-queen of diamonds and did not have the heart king. In that case he would falsecard by leading the diamond *queen*, trying to give the impression that East held the diamond king and, therefore, could not have the heart king.

So South decided against the finesse, put up the ace of hearts and made his contract, thus paying a very high-level and justified compliment to West's defensive powers as a falsecarder.

Insult an Opponent and He May Just Smile

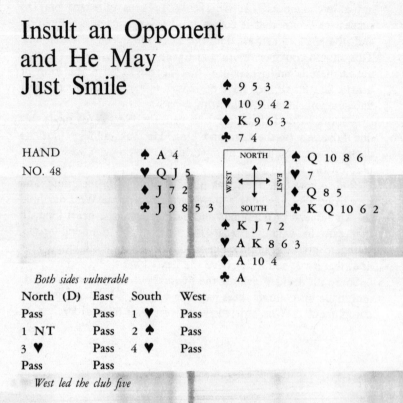

		♠ 9 5 3	
		♥ 10 9 4 2	
		♦ K 9 6 3	
		♣ 7 4	

HAND NO. 48

West		East
♠ A 4	NORTH	♠ Q 10 8 6
♥ Q J 5	WEST ← → EAST	♥ 7
♦ J 7 2		♦ Q 8 5
♣ J 9 8 5 3	SOUTH	♣ K Q 10 6 2

South:
♠ K J 7 2
♥ A K 8 6 3
♦ A 10 4
♣ A

Both sides vulnerable

North (D)	East	South	West
Pass	Pass	1 ♥	Pass
1 NT	Pass	2 ♠	Pass
3 ♥	Pass	4 ♥	Pass
Pass	Pass		

West led the club five

Insulting an opponent at the bridge table does not always lead to embarrassment and acrimony. It can sometimes be done, in a technical way, without the victim becoming aware of it. And if he is aware of the insult, he may be happy to be insulted.

Suppose that in the closing stages of the play you are able to force West to open up a suit that both sides would rather leave alone:

North
♦ K 9 6 3

South
♦ A 10 4

South needs to avoid losing a trick in the suit, and he assumes that each defender has at least three cards in it. He has no hope if East has both the missing honours, but if West has both, he will have to lead one, giving South the chance to win in his hand and finesse against West's remaining honour.

An inexperienced player sitting West will lead a small card if he has one honour. South captures East's honour, and finesses against West on the next round.

But if West is an expert, he will lead his honour from a holding such as J x x or Q x x. If South assumes that West has a queen-jack combination, he will fail. He should win in dummy and play for East to have the other honour.

If West leads an honour and an expert South wins in his own hand, he is offering West a subtle insult. The implication is that West is not a good enough player to lead an unsupported honour in this situation. But if West has led an unsupported honour, he will swallow the insult in exchange for a trick.

This situation arose in the diagrammed deal, which gave Edgar Kaplan of New York an opportunity to make a very fine play during the Spring National Championships in Cleveland in 1969. In a Vanderbilt Cup match against the eventual winners he found himself in a contract of four hearts, and the opening lead was the club five.

South took the club queen with the ace and played his two top trumps, hoping for a two-two division. When East showed out, he played a third trump. West won with the queen, and his only safe play was a club to East's king which South ruffed. Meanwhile East had discarded the two and six of clubs.

The obvious play was to use dummy's two entries for spade leads in the hope that East held A Q x in that suit. But South recognised that this was a remote chance. With such a spade holding in addition to a singleton heart and ♣ K Q 10 x x, East would no doubt have made a bid at some stage.

There was a much less obvious chance, and Kaplan played for it. Praying that West held a doubleton spade ace, he led a low spade from his own hand. East won the nine with the ten and returned the spade six. South put on the seven, and when West won with the ace, he was endplayed in this position:

```
                        NORTH
                        ♠ 5
                        ♥ 10
                        ♦ K 9 6 3
WEST                    ♣ -                       EAST
♠ -                                               ♠ Q 8
♥ -                                               ♥ -
♦ J 7 2                 SOUTH                      ♦ Q 8 5
♣ J 9 8                 ♠ K J                      ♣ 10
                        ♥ 8
                        ♦ A 10 4
                        ♣ -
```

A club lead would have allowed South to ruff in dummy and discard his losing diamond. So West led the diamond jack, hoping to look like a man making a cunning play with ♦ Q J x.

But Kaplan knew that West was an expert, and that West was twice as likely to have one diamond honour as two. So he won in dummy with the diamond king and finessed the diamond ten, claiming ten tricks when this play succeeded.

By uncovering the only line of play that offered a real chance of making the contract, South was able to gain 12 international match points for his team. He did not insult West by playing him to have both diamond honours: in the circumstances West would have been gratified by the insult.